FILLET FILLET
To Finish

An Awkward Journey to the Ironman

Trent Theroux

Fillet to Finish

By
Trent Theroux

ISBN-10: 1-946-30008-X
ISBN-13: 978-1-946-30008-9

1 2 3 4 5 6 7 8 9 10

Written by Trent Theroux
Cover Design by Dawn Porter
Published by Stillwater River Publications, Glocester, RI, USA.

*The views and opinions expressed in this book are solely those of the au-
thor and do not necessarily reflect the views and opinions of the pub-
lisher.*

Dedication

For my mother
who taught me that a good life
requires a good story.

"Any man's life, truly told, is a novel"

- Ernest Hemmingway
Death in the Afternoon

Acknowledgements

Thank you to my editor, Rich Salit – you hairy primate. Reteaching me the conventions of 5th grade English must have been an enormous burden to you." He said sarcastically. Your encouraging comments motivated me to work through the onslaught of red lines.

To my father – thank you for getting closer to me as we age. And thank you for wasting your time watching swim meets and baseball games.

To Haley & Max – thank you for always being in my thoughts and giving me the will to live and walk.

To Jill Lancaster – thank you for listening to each of these stories again and again as if it were for the first time. Thank you also for your ability to make me giggle and try new vegetables.

To Jane Theroux – thank you for teaching me how to swim and starting my journey. I miss Echo Lake.

To John Greene – thank you for seeing talent in a Boy Scout and telling his parents. Your dedication to the development of young men in Bristol, RI is admirable.

To Gail Alofsin – thank you for rekindling the fire to write this story.

To Lee Dilton-Hill and Pamela Ashe – thank you for helping me shape the story. I didn't appreciate that I suffered from "tunnel vision" until each of you lit the way.

In memory of Eugene McCarthy – thank you for teaching me the greatest business lesson in life.

Chapter One

The halo around the full moon was clear and vibrant. That was the first thing I saw when I came to the surface. A full moon lit the sky like a spotlight.

I was floating alone in the dark waters of Narragansett Bay, wondering how much blood I was losing through the slashes carved into my back by the boat's propeller. *I am in trouble. I am in serious, fucking trouble.* I repeated those words like a mantra while I watched the boat that ran over me motor away. Breathing at an erratic, almost frantic pace, I slowed my gasps as I tried to process exactly what had happened. Within a minute, I went from enjoying a night of vigorous exercise in my yellow sea kayak to holding my hand against the open wound in my back and touching what I thought was an exposed rib.

Across Narragansett Bay, Providence's two tallest skyscrapers were silhouetted by a glowing downtown skyline. To the west, residential street lamps looked like strands of twinkling Christmas tree lights. I bobbed in the water, still dazed by the events of the last few minutes, and fearful that if I closed my eyes I would slip underwater for good. My left arm did not respond when I attempted to swim to the nearby shore. Neither did my legs. With only my right arm, I struggled to stay afloat. The thought that my children could find me washed up dead on the shore began to haunt me. New Englanders are quite familiar with the news reports of fishermen lost at sea. Thirty-second news snippets detailed the boat they were in, the catch they were after, and the tearful loved ones left behind. Never had I thought much about the fishermen. Nor had I ever cared about the nightly news. Those tragic news items never bothered me until I envisioned my children crying in front of the unsympathetic camera.

In late September, the bay water was still warm and without any chop. I tried to get a bearing on where I was in the bay. Had I moved much? Was the current ebbing or flowing? Upper Narragansett Bay has several peninsulas to the southeast, including Bullocks Point, Adams Point, and Rumstick Point. Thousands of people lived in beautiful homes on the bay. Thousands of picture windows faced me. But at nine o'clock at night, I may as well have been in the Black Forest. People were not enjoying their premium views on this clear Monday night. Not that anyone would have noticed anything out of the ordinary. Just another Bayliner heading towards Bullocks Cove to dock at Lavin's Marina. That was probably all the residents of the eastern shores of

Narragansett Bay would have seen. Perhaps they would have heard the faint cries for help after the boat passed. Maybe.

I tried to yell for the boat to turn around, but my lungs were filled with seawater. I coughed to clear them, but the coughing sent pain through my back and legs. I kept trying to touch the gashes in my back as if I could heal them with the salt water. Farther and farther, the boat distanced itself from me and with it my hopes of getting out of the water. The eastern shore was at least two hundred yards away, maybe more; it was difficult to tell with only my head out of the water. As a competitive college swimmer, two hundred yards to shore was like crossing the street. Back then, I could have made the swim in less than two minutes, even without the flip turns, but that was fifteen years ago. Stranded in the water, injured, I sensed that I only had a few minutes to save myself and I had just wasted one of those precious minutes futilely calling after the boat that had motored away from me.

My kayak was floating to the south, towards where the bay opens wide on its way to Newport. My only salvation was to swim eastward. A line of streetlights outlined an old-money street in Barrington's Nayatt Point area. I envisioned the swim. With one arm, I could probably make it to shore in ten minutes, but I might bleed out before then. The dark water held the secret of how much or little blood I was losing. But, judging from the depth of the lacerations in my back, I figured my blood was gushing into the bay frighteningly fast. Even if I could make it to shore, then what? My legs were limp in the water. How would I traverse the rocky shore and reach the front door of one of mansions on their 50,000-square-foot lots? Would anyone answer the doorbell at this time of the night, especially without seeing the lights of someone's car pull into their circular driveway? Did I need to break a window just to get someone's attention and hope that they'd call 911? The most compelling question that raced through my mind was what if I did all that, but picked a house where no one was home? Would I have the strength to go to another house, or I would I fall like one of those tragic movie characters and just go to sleep? Still, I had the sense to know that my only hope of surviving was to get out of the water and get out fast. I started the one-armed swim towards shore.

The progress was excruciatingly slow. My one good arm was able to ferry my body through the water, but at a lethargic rate. Salt water still partially filled my lungs and my movement slowed even more when I was forced to cough out water. The pain from the cough was agonizing and with each hack I would drop just a little under the waterline.

From under the water, I could hear the sound of the boat's engine revving. I paused and peered into the darkness. I could just about see that the Bayliner had turned around. The boat had turned towards the west before motoring south back down the bay, but it didn't follow the same path as it had when heading toward the marina. A wave of relief overcame me. Relief that I might get out of this black trap. The feeling of deliverance was fleeting as I was without a way to signal to the captain. My kayak was floating south down to the heart of the bay and my paddle was somewhere unknown. Besides, the boat was now traveling a hundred yards west, farther away from me. Its pace now was not as swift as when it had struck me. The craft seemed to be trolling more than traveling. There was a small spotlight lighting a speck of the bay, but that light would never find me. I yelled a few times and the effort sent shock waves down my back. My lungs weren't filling with air, as they should, and I was left with a weakened voice.

The boat continued to travel closer, but still on a parallel line, never veering. After several minutes, it passed my position traveling south and I thought I had missed my opportunity. If the captain turned back up the bay to the west, he would never see me. My only chance of being spotted was if he turned to the east, towards the shore, on his return trip. My deflated confidence weakened as the captain steered his boat farther south. How would he ever see me? I was just a head bobbing in the water at night, invisible. The thought occurred to me that he might see the kayak and move towards it. Now I wasn't sure where the kayak was nor was I sure that it was any closer to me than the boat was. The darkness of night, my loss of blood, and the sea were playing tricks on my mind. How many more minutes did I have before I bled out? If I were standing on the ground, I could measure the amount of blood coming out of my body. But underwater, what's the difference? Blood – seawater. There was no way of telling.

The boat turned towards the east and started heading in my general direction. I used most of my remaining strength to call out to the boat and wave with my right arm. I wasn't able to wave for long because I couldn't keep my head above the water line without my right arm. With each desperate effort, my head dipped below the surface. The boat continued to move closer to me. Closer and closer it came, but without any sign that the captain had spotted me, or that he was even looking for me. Finally, hope came in the form of a sudden bright light. A spotlight was pointed right in my face. I had been found! The boat swung around so that I was facing its stern, and I made my way to the ladder at the back. A man reached into the water and grabbed me by my t-shirt. Using my last ounce of strength, I pulled up the ladder steps with my good arm. The men in the boat were swearing at me, four of them all yelling and cursing. I stared at them as my vision blurred, and collapsed facedown on a table in the back of the boat. Looking at my exposed back, they stopped yelling. One of the men went to the wheel, turned the boat around and headed towards Lavin's Marina. While he was driving, he called 911 and informed them that there was a boat accident and that a rescue truck would be needed at the marina. The other three men huddled around me trying to see if I was still conscious. They reeked of beer. I retained consciousness, and though exhausted, I was aware of everything being said. In fact, I was even more alert of my surroundings. Passing the coastline of Allin's Cove, I could see our modest Cape Cod house on Narragansett Avenue. The lights were out and it was dark inside. The boat turned away from the cove and into Lavin's Marina. I could see the flashing lights of the police and rescue vehicles on the landing as the driver navigated his boat into an open slip.

The rescue workers strapped me facedown to a backboard and put my head into the padded cradle at the top. The positioning reminded me of how I'd prepare for a backrub at the spa, but the throbbing in my back snapped me back to reality. As the rescue workers lifted me up and started to carry me away from the Bayliner, I grabbed the pant leg of one of the workers and pointed to the bottom of the boat. The entire floor was littered with empty, cheap domestic beer cans. I counted over forty of them as the rescue workers strapped me facedown onto a backboard. Fortunately my senses were still with me, and my wits as well.

Two rescue workers carried me off the boat. They walked slowly down the uneven dock towards the main pier. At the intersection with the main pier, I could see a policeman issuing a field sobriety exam to the boat's captain. The captain followed the policeman's physical instructions, but I couldn't pick up on any conversation between them.

After I was loaded into the rescue wagon, I asked one of the workers to use his cell phone to call my wife. He handed me his phone after I was strapped in. It was close to 10 p.m., and if Jennifer was still awake, I imagined she'd be going stir-crazy waiting for me to get home. If Jennifer was asleep, my call was going to seriously rattle her. Either way, I had the feeling that we both were going to be in for a long night.

Before I made the call, I took a few deep breaths to calm myself down. The rescue worker was tending to the wounds on my back and I needed to focus and communicate to Jennifer without emotion. My home phone was ringing and Jennifer answered with an agitated voice. I paused.

"I was in an accident," I said, trying to be as monotone and as emotionless as I could. "I'm all right. The rescue workers are taking me to the emergency room as a precaution. You should ask your mom to come to the house to watch the kids and meet me at Rhode Island Hospital."

I ended the call and dropped my head back into the padding. For the first time since the initial accident, I was starting to feel tremendous pain. The ambulance rolled forward and I listened to the blaring sound of the sirens. My eyes fluttered and a wave of exhaustion rushed over me. I began to relax and tried to put the sound of the siren far away from me. The ride to the hospital may have taken minutes or it may have taken hours. I couldn't be sure, as my mind was still swimming in the bay. I imagined the cars pulling over to the side of the road allowing us to pass while I was trying to understand what exactly happened. Trying to recall how I went from a peaceful evening of kayaking to an ambulance trip to the state's only Level 1 trauma center, Rhode Island Hospital.

My mind started replaying the events of the past few hours, trying to make sense of why I was lying face down in an ambulance. Fragments of memories flooded me and they were difficult to organize.I was jarred back to the present as the ambulance driver took a sharp right turn and stopped abruptly. The rear door opened. The driver was joined by two other men in blue dressing gowns holding each the side of a rolling stretcher.

The EMT inside the cabin with me released the straps that had secured me, and then he and the other men loaded me onto the stretcher, still with the backboard under me. With great haste the hospital attendants pushed me through the emergency room doors. And, I could only wonder, how much blood have I lost? Why can't I move my left arm and why can I still not feel my legs?

Chapter Two

I was born and raised in Rhode Island, never far from the water. I body surfed, quahogged, clammed, raced, floated, and splashed in beaches throughout the Ocean State. I walked, watched sunsets, built sandcastles, flew kites, fished, and climbed rocks along its many miles of coastline. I loved the water.

My mother took me to Third Beach as a young child and I played in the sand and surf all day, not unlike most kids raised in that area. I kissed my high school sweetheart for the first time on the shoreline of the bay. At fifteen, I swam my first open-water race, from Rumstick Point to Colt State Park. My friends from the Boy Scouts threw seaweed at me as they paddled my escort canoe. I would drive my wife and kids to Flo's in Island Park for chowder and clam cakes. We would take our lunch over the seawall and put our toes in the Sakonnet River. On special occasions, we would order fried clams. I loved the water.

I had spent over ten hours in the office that Monday in late September 2002, and I was itching for a little exercise. There had been a gorgeous full moon two nights previous, and I decided to paddle my yellow kayak out into the bay. I threw on a pair of beat up shorts, ditched my dress shirt in favor of my white undershirt, grabbed my MP3 player and headed out the door. We had bought the kayak late in the summer and I'd taken a shine to riding in the early evening after the children went to bed. Our house was close to Allin's Cove; I needed to cross a small section of my neighbor Miss Dottie's property to get to the kayak. The late-September bay water was warm. The full moon was bright enough for me to see the Conimicut lighthouse, over a mile away and down into Warwick. I put out into the upper bay.

On my way out to Nayatt Point, I saw just one boat, the Providence to Newport ferry. The high-speed ferry was cruising south down the channel and I had the brief thought that I was glad not to have been too close because of the boat's wake. The initial wake from the ferry was over a quarter-mile away, but now there were tiny waves just strong enough to rock me gently in the kayak. I made the turn at Nayatt Point, which was about a mile and a half from Allin's Cove. It took nearly twenty minutes for me to reach the turnaround point as I was aided by the current. Now, heading back north towards home, I could feel the tug of the current and a whisper of a breeze in my face.

Monday Night Football played on my MP3 headset and Kurt Warner was leading the St. Louis Rams towards the end zone when I felt vibrations in the water. Knowing it was nighttime, and I was less visible in the kayak, I was more sensitive to boats out in the bay.

A few hundred yards directly behind me, I saw a boat heading up the bay in my general direction. It was the only boat I noticed, save for the ferry, which had passed ten or more minutes ago. Why was the boater coming in this direction? I wasn't in the channel. Where was he headed? It is amazing how fast one's synapses can fire when under mounting pressure. Soldiers in combat must be constantly assessing threats and creating decision rules. And they'd have the proper training to keep their wits about them to act decisively. Would the boat swerve out of my path and away from me? On my way out to Nayatt Point, I had spotted a group of fishermen parked in their boat and drinking near the Conimicut lighthouse. Maybe they were going to buzz by and make me roll over in their wake. Maybe? The boat was getting closer. It was up on plane and moving straight towards me at a decent clip. How much time was left before they'd hit me? Ten, fifteen seconds? Maybe? I twisted my torso around in the kayak and waved my paddle in the air, trying to get them to notice me. My seven-foot long paddle was making small arcs in the air. The boat held its course and was coming dead at me. The moonlight was shining and very bright. I could see for several miles past them, and I was in a yellow boat waving a huge white stick. They *had* to be able to see me. Why were they still coming at me? Fear engulfed me. I was about to be hit.

I steered a little to the left, but I couldn't move out of the path. The boat was going to hit me right in the chest. I was a dead man. It would hit me in the chest and decapitate me. The only way to avoid this happening was to get under the boat. But what was its draft? Two feet? Three feet? I should be able to drop that deep in a second or two. Maybe? Hopefully?? I rolled out of the kayak and tried to push my legs against the bottom to gain some leverage. Unfortunately, when the kayak flipped I was only kicking it into the air. I swept my arms through the water in a breaststroke pull. Again, I pulled deeper. The hum of the engine was upon me. Its spine-chilling roar was much louder in the ocean than above the surface. The noise was thunderous in my ears.

Then the unthinkable happened. The boat hit me. A 3,500-pound mass of fiberglass flying through the water at over 25 mph struck me squarely in the middle of my back. The sensation was like being tackled by a large, fast linebacker. It knocked the wind out of me but did not hurt me. Surprisingly, the pain wasn't terrible. But any hope I had of having just escaped serious injury was dashed as the propeller started carving the skin, muscles and bones in my back. My back was prone when the propeller started slicing. Like a fish on a cutting board, the propeller filleted me in four successive cuts from the center left side of my back straight down to my butt. Each whack from the propeller felt like being struck by a powerful man swinging a two-by-four. Again and again and again and again. For good measure, I received a fifth scrape from some metal along the boat's bottom.

The boat continued motoring on as if nothing had happened. Even with the Doppler effect, I could hear the scream of the engine. It appeared to be laughing as it roared away. I was dazed, somewhere under the water and not sure where the surface was. I opened my eyes. The water was black. Normally, I'd follow the bubbles, but they were invisible. My air was all but gone. The deep breath I took rolling out of the kayak was practically expended. The breaststroke pulls consumed some air. The boat's assault knocked the balance out of me. I stopped moving and felt myself sink in what I assumed was toward the bottom. I was so tired. My mind was drained and I wanted to just close my eyes. I breathed, just a nip, took in some seawater and my lungs began to burn. The fire was painful and ignited my senses. I tried to kick my legs, but they did not respond. During my high school and college swimming years, I must have kicked over 500 miles, but now when I needed to kick ten measly feet to the surface, they wouldn't respond.

The blackness of the water engulfed me. From a few feet below the surface, the sky was invisible, as distant as the next planet. My good arm instinctively began to pull my body to the surface. It pulled in long, sweeping strokes – just as I had practiced for thousands of hours in my youth.

Chapter Three

Twenty years ago, when I was seventeen, I was rushed into the same hospital's emergency room following a car accident. I remembered seeing the faces of the nurses, the long corridors between the old building's rooms and the new building's bright rows of sterile fluorescent lights. Now, I can see nothing as I am face down on a pad and my head is strapped to the backboard. The paramedics wheeled me into the hospital, transferred me and my backboard to some male nurses, who passed me to a doctor or a nurse. All the while, I had the sensation of spinning stomach-down on a playground swing. Someone wheeled me into a very spacious room with a slab in the center. The slab reminded me of the stone table from *The Lion, the Witch and the Wardrobe*. For some reason, I could hear the fawns in the distance hiding from the White Witch, fearing they would be turned into stone. Two more nurses lifted me out of the gurney, straining themselves, and plopped my 200-pound body facedown onto the stone table.

Jennifer met me in the slab room within minutes of my arrival. She had been crying, but I could see in her eyes that she was trying to regain her strength and composure. Not knowing exactly what had happened to me must have led her to vividly imagine why I told her to drop everything and come to the hospital. Jennifer and I were married nearly nine years ago. The man she saw leaving for work that morning was fit, in his mid-thirties, with brown (formerly blond) hair, fair skin and nearly-blue eyes. I imagine she wasn't at all prepared to see me lying on the slab, cut open like a piece of bloody meat.

Nurses scurried in and out of the room, checking devices and meters outside of my view. Some talked to Jennifer – others ignored us. One nurse asked me what my level of pain was. Frankly, it was pretty low. Shock from the accident must have still been protecting me. Then she took out a pair of scissors and began to cut open the back of my shorts. She sheared through the rear seam and through my underwear to completely expose my body. I was naked and cold on the table. Jennifer pleaded that I be given something to cover myself with, but she was rebuffed.

"We need to irrigate him first," the nurse said.

Irrigated? That didn't sound good at all.

Within a few minutes, the nurse returned and explained what irrigation was. Because of the high levels of bacteria in the ocean and the even higher levels concentrated on the propeller, they needed to flush me out to avoid infection following surgery.

"There is only one way to remove the algae and contaminants," she said.

Unfortunately, it wasn't much more sophisticated than a car wash. They were about to aim a hose at my open wounds and blast the area with a high-pressured solution.

"You might want to grip tightly onto the edge of the table," she said. "I'm going to try and make this as easy as possible. But it's going to hurt."

Years later, I can still remember the agonizing pain of the irrigation. The nurse turned the hose on and applied the spray to the upper cut on my back, the shallowest. The pressurized water stabbed my open wound and exposed nerves. The water moved down my back to the deeper wounds. My eyes lost focus and the room turned white. My senses were absolutely exploding with pain. My right hand clutched the stone table and my left constricted around Jennifer's smaller hand, as if I were trying to transfer some of the pain to her. A low, dull moan emanated from deep within my chest, a sound that I have never heard before in my life. It made me think of an old farmhouse door opening slowly.

The flushing continued. The spray was moving back and forth along the largest gash, pelting me like machine-gun fire. Ultimately, my mind or my body succumbed to the pain and shut down. Everything was black and I was under the water again.

I awoke to a bright white light, the beeps of machinery, and water under my stomach. The nurses had left the room and the hose was off. Someone had placed a heated blanket or towel on my back, but my stomach was cold and wet. I could hear Jennifer talking in the hallway in muted tones. I tried to follow the one-sided conversation, but my chattering teeth distracted me from listening. Consciousness was at the end of an ever-lengthening tunnel, visible but entirely unreachable. My eyes fluttered and closed involuntarily.

In this not-quite-conscious state, I was adrift at sea, floating on top of the water. The soft waves rocked me gently and the water grew warm lulling me into a deeper sleep. Subconsciously I knew I should awaken from this dream, but I was powerless to do so. I grew frightened about not being able to float without using my arms and legs, but I couldn't move my limbs to protect myself. The lapping of the water against my ears was replaced by a high-pitched hum. The humming was away in the distance, but the frequency was growing. A single engine's hum resonating in the warm water was getting closer to me. I couldn't see the boat but the hum became deafening. I screamed in my mind to wake up, but I couldn't escape the sound of the humming. My body was exhausted. My mind was frightened. I finally succumbed to the stress and passed out.

Chapter Four

As the effects of the morphine wore off, I started to feel more pain. I knew that I was lying in the hospital bed, unable to move, and I needed to focus on something. The best news was that I lived through the night. The worst news was that I lived through the night but could not move or feel my legs. The morning doctor called my name several times from the middle of my quad-patient hospital room, waiting for one of the four patients to acknowledge him. Morphine has a way of blocking your ears even when someone is standing right in front of you calling your name. The doctor stroked the soles of my feet with a tongue depressor and flicked his little hammer on my knees.

"Imm gnnn rawk," I said.

For those of you who have not had the pleasure of being doped up on morphine, I had just said, "I'm going to walk." The doctor shushed me while he made notes in his folder. Doctors in the hospital are always doing that, telling patients to shush, relax, or be quiet. Doctors want every conversation to be one-sided. They talk - you listen. The patient should speak only when told to speak. God forbid the patient should use any polysyllabic words or the doctor will just tell them to relax.

"Imm gnnn rawk." *I'm going to walk.*

"Just relax."

"I'm going to walk, then I'm…"

"Shhh. You need to save your strength."

I didn't want to save my strength. This shushing buffoon failed to grasp the gravity of what I was telling him. I was going to walk again. At that point, I had no idea how easy or challenging it would be, but if the complete lack of sensation in my legs was any indication, it was not a good one.

The doctor was telling Jennifer something and I could tell by the rigidity of her body that she was preparing for or processing bad news. I couldn't make out her face clearly because I could see three of them and I was trying to focus on the middle one. She wasn't crying like she was last night when they laid me on the slab, but she was working hard to push out the emotions and try to focus on what the doctor was saying.

Looking out the window, I could see the sun was already high in the sky. Was it still morning or had we passed to afternoon? The doctor left and Jennifer came to the side of my bed and stroked my hand. The tears she fought off while listening to the doctor came pouring out.

We were both scared. Jennifer told me that the doctors were unsure about the severity of the damage to my spinal cord. We knew that the cord was not severed. It would be a few days before we knew the extent of the damage. Until that point, we needed to wait. She told me that I had been in surgery for nearly five hours. The only thing I remember from the operating room was asking for the doctor to look into my eyes and tell me that I was going to see my wife and kids again. Jennifer then described the damage the propellers did to my back. There were four deep lacerations, two of which were down to the rib cage. It took hundreds of stitches to reattach the muscles in successive layers. The skin was stapled together and a protective covering was placed over the top. Five pieces of my spinal column were cut out by the propellers. Their primary concern was my spinal cord. I could live a normal, but different life with the rest of the damage. We both sat in silence digesting the information. Stitches, staples, carved.

Jennifer left shortly afterwards to check on our children and get some much-needed sleep. I closed my eyes but could only see black. The water surrounded me and I was slipping under.

"You okay, Papi?"

I heard the voice, but didn't recognize where it was coming from.

"You okay, Papi?"

It was a sweet, tender, young voice. It came from behind a curtain in the bed diagonally across from me. I asked who it was.

"Angel."

The voice had a thick Latino accent. It sounded like "An-hell." Angel talked and I listened, not understanding a word. He talked and his soothing voice and nonsensical words took me out of the water and I drifted off to sleep.

"Papi, you okay?"

I woke up and felt a stickiness on my cheeks. I must have been crying in my sleep.

"You okay, Papi?"

"I'm okay, Angel. I'll be okay. You okay, Angel?"

"No."

He started weeping and I drifted back to sleep, hitting the morphine button every few seconds.

The morning doctor woke me the next day by abruptly pulling my eyelids open. The Samsonite gorilla is gentler on luggage than this guy was on a human body. He poked me, rocked me a little, then used his tongue depressor against my toes. No sensation. He marked notes in a file and left. Thirty-six hours had passed since I was sliced open and I still didn't have feeling in my toes.

"You okay, Angel?"

"*Si*. You okay, Papi?"

"I'm scared. I don't know if I'll be able to walk out of this room."

I began to cry silently.

Soon after, the nurses came to see Angel and they pulled back the curtain to reveal a young man, a teenager of maybe sixteen. He flashed me a bright smile as we looked at each other for the first time. Until that moment, I felt like we were passing notes in prison. Now, I could feel his humanity. The nurses lifted him out of bed and helped him into the bathroom from which emanated a litany of moans and cries. They brought Angel back to bed. He lay in his bed and we stared at each other. He pointed to himself, put his hands together and mimicked swinging a baseball bat.

"Baseball," he said.

I smiled. I pointed to myself and swung my imaginary bat.

"Baseball," I said. "Red Sox."

"Yankees," he said, pointing at himself.

I gave the sick kid a pass on that one. The nurses pulled the curtain around his bed. Ten minutes passed and I was still glowing over our brief encounter.

"You okay, Angel?"

"*Si.*"

"You okay, Papi?"

"*Si.*"

Jennifer came to visit. There was no medical news to discuss, so we spent the time talking about the children's day at school and what she was going to make them for dinner. I did more listening than talking. I didn't feel the need to press the morphine plunger once. My body, or my mind was starting to accept. When Jennifer left, I asked that she get me something from the Walmart down the street.

The food was better than I expected. Then again, I never complain about a free meal. The nurses did their poking and prodding shortly after I finished my meal and continually tried to brighten my spirits. The evening doctor came in for his rounds. This chap was certainly a kinder, gentler version of the morning Marquis de Sade. He rubbed my legs, asked me about my general feeling and how often I was hitting the morphine plunger. Then, a spark! I felt his fingers on my toes. It was unclear if the feeling was real or my imagination, so I asked the doctor to press harder. It was real! I could feel him squeezing my big toe. Not since my mother blew kisses on my toes had anything felt so wonderful to me. The doctor continued his examination and commented that there was no movement, but that sensation was the first step. Wow!

My mindset changed instantly. The List I had made in my mind started to roll in front of my eyes, like the opening lines to *Star Wars*. I could see each of the items I wanted to accomplish and I could visualize myself completing each. The doctor snapped me back to attention. He could see that I had just exited to the movie editing room and told me that I should temper my expectations until more tests were completed.

Jennifer came back to the room later with a Walmart bag for me. She was immediately in tears when I told her the news of my big toe sensations. We discussed the endless possibilities of what it could mean. I opened the bag, took out the brand new baseball Jennifer bought and asked her for a pen to write. I signed my name to the ball - "Papi Trent" and asked Jennifer to bring it to Angel, whose curtain had been drawn back for the afternoon. His grin reached the ceiling as he rolled the ball over in his hands. He pointed to the name then to me.

"Papi."

I nodded. I watched him with the ball and wished I could hit two home runs for him.

Nighttime came along with another more-than-decent dinner. The evening doctor squeezed my toes again. Again, I could feel the sensation. My hopes of a future with movement were brimming. The nighttime nurse took my tray and asked me if I needed to pee. I told her no. In fact, I hadn't thought about peeing since I'd arrived at the hospital. She told me that I had taken in a lot of fluids and that it was getting time to relieve my bladder. Either I peed on my own by morning or the nurses would help me pee, promptly dashing my enthusiasm. Help me pee? What type of hell? Oh, gosh! I knew what was coming.

Chapter Five

*B*ANG! RIP! BANG! BEEP! BEEP! BEEP! I was awakened suddenly in the middle of the night by strange sounds. I was dazed and confused until I saw a half-dozen people in the room scrambling to find something along the floor of Angel's bed. The lights above his bed were on and a man whose head was silhouetted by bright white light shouted forceful commands. A male nurse wheeled a rolling bed into the room and a team of workers in white coats lifted Angel off his bed onto the roller. He was limp and seemed unaffected by the jostling from one position to another. As quickly as the team had charged into the room, they retreated. The last person shut off Angel's light and fixed his pillow. It was dark again and I was sore. I didn't know what ailed Angel. I hoped he would be all right. Earlier, Jennifer had inquired about Angel and found out that he had had sections of his colon removed. And apparently, it wasn't the first time he had surgery in that area. Now I saw why he seemed so frail. Jennifer told me that he'd said he had suffered since he was a child. I didn't know where Angel went, or if he was still alive. I squeezed the morphine plunger and in a few minutes lapsed back into the dark water and a fitful sleep.

The morning nurse came in a couple of minutes after I woke up to a sunny morning. She was chipper as she inspected the clipboard at my bedside and read the notes that had been recorded on my medical records. Then she took my vitals. Jennifer was already in the room and they chatted about working long hours, the weather, and other small talk. When the nurse was finished, she asked if I needed to pee. I said no. She went to the closet and took out a kidney-shaped plastic pail. She moved my legs apart and placed the pail between my legs. She told me to relax, to think about peeing, and she would be back in a few minutes. How does one think about peeing? I tried the normal river-flowing crap, but it was of no use to me. I couldn't focus on anything that would help me pee. I tried to think of the time in my life when I needed to pee the most: childhood days sitting in Sunday Mass; during a timed portion of my SAT; during my best friend's wedding. Then, I thought of the one time I needed to pee the most.

I was seventeen and in a room just a few floors below the room I was in at the moment. I had an overnight stay in the hospital following a car accident. I had lost a lot of blood before coming into the hospital so I was receiving a constant IV drip. That, coupled with the fact that I had drunk six or seven ginger ales before I got to the hospital made my bladder as fragile as a water balloon. I remembered telling a nurse that I needed to pee and she had replied that I could not get away from the bed because I was hooked up to monitors and IVs. She left the room and promptly returned with a lemonade jar. It was plastic and had markings for ounces lining the outside of the jar. The nurse handed me the container and curtly left the room. I stood up, opened the jar and began to relieve the pressure.

The flow was of great relief for only a few seconds before panic began to set in. The bottle was filling rapidly. I had previously inserted "myself" into the bottle's aperture to minimize any spillage and now withdrew "myself" to make room for a few more ounces. The urine was rising to the top of the bottle and I was leaking. I tried to close off my internal valve but that sent a wave of uncomfortableness to the part of my body that was not accustomed to uncomfortableness. I took a quick scan around the room and noticed both the trashcan and the sink. I might be able to reach the trashcan without popping my IV. The sink was entirely too far away. My mind was working to conjure up a story I would need to explain to the janitor as to why the trash can was full of piss. I suspected that conversation would not go well for me. I made a brave move towards the sink. The IV restrained me for only a second as I pulled the needle out of my arm. I reached the edge of the sink and released the pressure. Relief coursed through me as the remaining waste exited my body. "Hmmmmmmm." I matched the gentle hum I heard in the room as I finished my work and started to shake out the balance.

Just then, the door burst open and a doctor and nurse pushing an A/V tray complete with electronic paddles came charging into my room, expecting to find a Code Blue. My face whitened in terror as I stood with my dick in my hand over the sink. My God! Is this what they do to sinners in this hospital?

I snapped out of my daydream still without the sensation or ability to pee.

"Trent," the nurse told me, "it's time to pee."

"I just can't do it."

I could hear the humiliation in my voice. I was unable to control my bodily functions. The morning nurse nodded and left the room, and the kidney-shaped bowl still lay between my legs, empty. Several minutes later, the morning nurse returned with two other nurses. "Nurses" might be an exaggeration given the way they strutted into my room. One was cut from the same cloth as the prototypical lunch lady. She lacked shape, but rather was a block of a woman, granite from her neck to her shoes. The other had a chin that could saw a log. She was slighter than the first, but not some waif under her dress whites. There was a sense of impending doom moving through the air in the room. The morning nurse told me that she wanted to see if gravity would help the situation. The two linebackers were going to lift me from the bed and hopefully the pee would start to flow. This would be my first time out of bed and I was terrified of how my legs and back would respond. The nurses looked strong on the outside, but I was a 200-pound slab of meat without any motor controls.

The morning nurse gently rolled me onto my side, exposing my back to Jennifer and the sunlight. Following my surgery, the surgeon had applied a long sheet of transparent adhesive strip to my back to protect the stitches and staples. I thought it felt like flypaper. Jennifer thought it looked like parchment paper. The morning nurse then moved my legs towards the edge of the bed and with the help of one of the other nurses seated me on the bed. The two yokozunas each put one of my arms around their shoulders and lifted. I was standing! Check that. They propped me up. My feet were touching the ground, but without the sensation of standing yet. My legs were unsure of the floor, as if I were afraid the linoleum tiles would suddenly melt under me.

After what seemed like an eternity, but was just fifteen or twenty seconds, I started to allow more weight to be borne by my legs. I was heavy, but not applying more than twenty pounds of weight on the ground. The nurses held the rest. The morning nurse handed the kidney pail to Chinzilla who, in turn, put her hand and the pail under my johnnie. Hello!

"How long does this take to work?" I asked.

"Normally, a minute or so. You've suffered significant trauma and your system has shut down to protect itself. We hope to see some flow shortly."

Jennifer was getting a kick out of this. She and I eyeballed each other with that type of non-verbal communication only shared between the closest of friends. She knew exactly what I was thinking. In all the fantasies that every man has ever had throughout the entire history of civilization, including Cro-Magnon man, having your penis held by two nurses ranks no lower than number three! I didn't care that these two women were late for their post time at Belmont. They had on the right uniform for my fantasy. I closed my eyes and started to shoot video for my personal highlight reel.

The morning nurse interrupted my editing session.

"It's time for you to go," she said.

With that, she took control of the kidney pail, wrapped her fingers around my penis and started to shake me to help the urine flow. I could not believe my eyes. A third nurse joined in the escapade.

"Do you know how much I would have to pay for this type of action in Vegas?" I said to Jennifer in a voice that was much too loud. She was practically on the floor now. "Listen, there is a bar being raised to a whole new level in the bedroom following this."

For the first time since my accident, I actually laughed and, involuntarily, I put a little more weight on the floor.

The party stopped when the morning nurse decided that her valiant efforts were not working. The team moved me back into the bed and cantered out of the room.

"You're going to want that treatment going forward, I presume?" Jennifer said.

"Every day of my life," I replied. "You'd better go out and buy a few good uniforms."

The morning nurse returned a few minutes later with a more serious look on her face. The happy lines around her round forehead were replaced with a worried frown.

"Have you ever been catheterized, Trent?"

"No," I said.

In fact, the only time I even saw a catheter was during my senior year of high school. As part of my Catholic high school education, students were required to perform

Christian service. I chose to help at St. Joseph's Hospital in Providence; coincidentally, I was born at St. Joseph's. Students worked a three-hour shift, one day a week for twelve weeks, assisting the hospital staff in any way they could, but mostly the staff wanted us to interact with some of the patients. The smell of the hospital was dank as opposed to antiseptic and had an aura of being a place to die rather than be healed.

St. Joseph's Hospital looked tired. The paint was crumbling in places along the corridor walls and the colors were straight out of black and white movies. The staff left medical equipment outside doors and in corners like rusted heaps in a junkyard. Walking down my assigned hallway required slalom-like skills to avoid hitting some type of beeping apparatus. My supervisor assigned me to the west corridor of the third floor and told me that I was to visit the patients and try to talk with them. Generally, try to keep the patients in good spirits, I was instructed. This was a plum assignment considering I half-expected Brother Anthony to schedule me in the morgue for using the Lord's name in vain earlier in the week.

My rounds over my first few weeks were more enjoyable than I anticipated. Most patients were new each time I visited and they were generally appreciative of a happy face talking with them and killing time. I never asked the patients what ailment brought them to the hospital and, thankfully, most didn't offer. The patients and I mostly talked about the weather and the coming of spring. Christian service was proving to be an easy A for the 3rd quarter.

A new patient had arrived during my fourth week. The man was older, probably in his eighties, completely bald except for wisps of white hair around his temples. His eyes were gray and tired. He had the look of a man who had finished what he'd come to do and was ready for a rest. He did not reciprocate my smile nor my greeting. The orderly told me that the man was "Greek or something" and didn't speak English. That was fine. He didn't have to talk. He just needed to listen. I described the coming of spring and the beginning of spring training for the Red Sox and other whimsical topics for the next ten minutes. Then I said my goodbye and left.

The following week, Zorba -- I secretly nicknamed all of my patients -- was in the exact same spot where I'd left him the previous week. My conversation was the same and his lack of response was the same, too. This routine continued for two more visits. I tried to enlighten Zorba as to why *this* was the year for the Red Sox. On that visit, a nurse came into the room carrying a clear plastic hose and a plastic bedpan. She laid the equipment on the bedside table, put on a pair of latex gloves and raised the tube for Zorba to see. Zorba offered the nurse the slightest, barely-perceivable of nods. It was as if Zorba was laying down his sword to his kingdom's conqueror. The nurse lifted his dressing gown, exposing his aged penis and atrophied legs. Just seventeen, I was taken aback and my stomach lurched at seeing his deteriorating body. I was not entirely sure what was going to happen here, but the scene was getting grotesque quickly. I turned to walk away out of the room when I felt the cold skin of Zorba's hand on mine. I faced the tired, old man. He stared at me with those ancient gray eyes, and I was unsure if he wanted me to stay or was giving me permission to leave. Ultimately, I watched the nurse insert the tube into the head of Zorba's penis. My eyes started to water as I imagined pain caused from this invasion. Zorba, though, had a peaceful look on his face. His wrinkled lines were relaxed, resigned to the submission of his body to the nurse. Within moments, urine flowed from the tube along with a noticeable amount of some red, viscous substance I assumed to be blood. The process took only a minute before the nurse extracted the tube, cleaned the area and left the room.

Zorba's face showed no signs of bother as if catheterization was as natural as the sunrise. Maybe it was old age, which deadened the spirits, leaving the body limp like a leaf on the sidewalk. Maybe he'd been poked and stabbed so many times that one more time didn't matter. Maybe it was the best way to take care of the body's needs.

I gave a resigned nod to the morning nurse and watched her lift my gown, and insert the tube into my penis. I blanched at the discomfort and looked within myself for peace. Within moments, I could feel the urine flowing out of my system and the natural relief of a good piss.

I had returned to the hospital the following week to continue my Christian service. My rounds were exciting as baseball season had begun and there was plenty to talk about including this new pitcher for the Red Sox, Roger Clemens. I stood outside the door to Zorba's room and reflected on the moment we had shared the previous week. For the first time, I felt like I made a spiritual connection, the kind of connection the Christian Brothers had told me might happen during my service tour. I ambled into the room and found an elderly woman lying in Zorba's bed. She was asleep and looked like she was about a hundred years old. The woman had tubes entering her body in various places and a monitor alongside her bed beeping with a slight drawl. An orderly entered the room while I was standing there.

"Excuse me, can you please tell me where the elderly gentleman who was here for the past few weeks has gone?"

The orderly told me that the man had died two days earlier, as she continued her work in the room.

My morning nurse removed the catheter. It felt like a long, slow needle was being removed from my vein. She took away my urine and her gear and left the room. I felt violated and embarrassed. I reached for the plunger and self-medicated. A minute later, my surgeon, Dr. Iannetti entered the room. The doctor reintroduced himself to me and, in very technical terms, described my injuries and the work he had performed. Although I wanted to listen intently, my mind kept replaying the sensation of the catheter being removed.

"And, there is a high probability that you will be able to walk again," he said.

My mind snapped back to attention.

"Walk? Like, walk?"

"Yes. We're not sure yet to what extent you will be able to walk, but yes, you should be able to walk again at some point."

My heart swelled and I felt reborn. I was going to walk. I was going to leave this hospital room. I thanked him. I thanked him. I thanked him.

Chapter Six

The List started simply: *walk*. I was going to get out of this bed and walk. The mental note, or conviction, came during the first evening. Jennifer went home for the evening to tend to the children, leaving me alone with my thoughts, the morphine, and the beeping of my Angel's machines. Walk. The doctor said that I would eventually walk. He was short on details as to how far I could walk or whether I would have any restrictions on my walking. He simply told me that *I would walk*. So, what's next?

How was I going to get out of the hospital? I would walk to the elevator, press the down arrow, get out, and walk to the car. So far, that was all in the category of walking. Eventually, I would need to climb the front stairs of the house and the stairs to our bedroom. I now had my second item on The List: *Climb a flight of stairs.* What's next?

There was a clatter in the hallway and a team of folks dressed in white rushed by, disturbing my train of thought. Suddenly, I thought of my kids. I missed Haley and Max. Haley, eight years old, was a powerful and assertive young girl. Max, three, was…a three-year-old boy. It was about this time of night that the horsey would put the kids to bed. On most nights, I would get on all fours in the living room and tell Max that the horse was ready to take him to bed. Max had the option of which horse he wanted to ride each night. On most nights, he would choose the sleepy, bucking horse, then climb onto my back. The horse never moved without a command. Some nights, Max would just sit there, not realizing that he needed to instruct me. He then would lean forward next to my ear and whisper in a low, Louisiana drawl, "Geaux." The horse would take off with something less than a canter. Without notice, the horse would fall asleep, just plop right on the ground and not move. Max would shake my back and shirt violently trying to get the horse to move. Sometimes he would grab the horse's ears, which got the horse to jump quickly. Once up, the horse would buck Max to the brink of him falling off, then just as quickly fall asleep again. Never to be left out, Haley would command Max on how best to ride me. She was getting too big to ride every night, but sometimes when the horse was feeling frisky she could get a chance. Haley would shout out the commands to Max between the sleeping and the bucking. The routine continued for ten minutes or until the horse needed oats, or a beer.

I missed my kids. I wanted to put them on my back and ride around the house and the whole town. *I want to lift my children again.*

My company had scheduled the rollout a new accounting system on Monday and I was the project manager. My team had worked on the project for nearly eight months and Monday was the day. We had lined up multiple vendors to coordinate the cutover and we had all of our in-house staff prepared for the change. Not that being unable to walk ever comes at a good time, but this was a really bad time. The project needed to be finished. My company depended on me. *I want to go back to work.*

I had a private TV in my hospital room. *Jeopardy!* was on with the sound off. "Nineteenth-century authors" was the category the contestants were trying to solve. My puzzles were more complex. What else did I want to solve? Where else did I want to go? My thoughts moved from the 19th century to the empty bed where Angel had slept. Where had they taken him? And, the baseball he had. I loved baseball. I loved all the clichés in baseball movies. Where did Angel go? I tried to think stronger thoughts and returned to The List.

I thought about Jennifer. She was heroic. She was showing signs of strain, but they were mild compared to the amount of stress I had caused her over the past two days. She was brave for both of us. I loved her. The imp who lives in my head and thinks the most perverse thoughts asked, "Are you going to be able to have sex with her again?" Dear God, I am a virile, sexually-obsessed man in his mid-thirties with decades of activities ahead. Can I have sex with her again? If the little episode with the catheter earlier this morning was any indication, then I had ridden my last boat to tuna town. The imp has a dirty sense of humor. *I want to have sex with my wife.*

Nothing. I expected the sexual thoughts to stir Lil' Trent into action, but he was unresponsive.

I grabbed a piece of paper from the desk and started to write out The List. Walk, climb a flight of stairs, lift my children, return to work, and make love to Jennifer. The List seemed like normal everyday life. Simple. Routine. My handwriting was poor. It normally is poor and the medication likely was contributing to the illegible scribble.

My kids had never seen the Red Sox. Haley saw the Pawtucket Red Sox when she was only three months old, which, come to think of it, irked me. I had attended dozens of Pawtucket and Boston Red Sox games over my lifetime. During my younger years, I would always carry a glove with me on the off chance a foul ball or a home run would venture my way. Only once did I have a halfway-decent shot of catching a foul ball, but I still would have needed to climb over three rows of fans to make the catch. My father holding me down by the seat of my pants dashed those aspirations. So, it was to my great annoyance that when Jennifer and I took Haley to her first game at three months old, the left fielder caught a foul ball right in front of us to end the inning and he handed the ball to…baby Haley. Grrrrrrr. Still, I would have loved to have the children watch Pedro Martinez pitch. *I want to take my kids to Fenway Park.*

Why was there a grizzly bear on the screen talking to a dog? You turn your head away for just a minute and you go from 19th-century authors to interspecies discussions. What was the bear talking about? I turned away and let my mind drift back to things I wanted to do with my life.

The first six seemed like they could be relatively easy -- assuming, and this was a big assumption, that I would be able to walk out of the hospital under my own power. If I could walk out on my own, what else would I wish to do? I was challenged because I had everything I could ask for: a good job, a loving wife, beautiful kids, a nice house, a wonderful community, my health...scratch. My health was in question.

My philosophy professor, who taught Aristotle in Western Civilization, said, "The unexamined life is not worth living." What is the unexamined life? Is it a job, a wife, kids, a house, a community? My studies lacked the focus I needed back then. Now, maybe there is more. Maybe I can cross a chasm and live with more challenge in my life. Most of what I had now came very easily to me. I was living the unexamined life, not having to work very hard to achieve the wonderful successes I enjoyed. Maybe I could push myself a little further. I searched my mind for a challenging physical activity, mainly because my mental acuity was unable to take down Gary Kasparov in speed chess. A marathon. I tried to run a marathon when I was younger, but quit on myself. To be fair, I trained for one day then quit. A marathon would be challenging. *I want to run a marathon.*

If I'm going to run marathons, I thought, I might as well climb mountains. Mount Everest seems like a good place to start. What was that saying? "Go big or go home." In this case, I would probably go home because I'm a pussy when it comes to the cold. Climbing mountains in the ice and snow is crazy, especially for someone who, at that moment, could not walk. However, climbing a mountain would be cool. I could visualize myself standing at the peak, viewing the top of the world, seeing the Himalayan mountain range stretching for miles in every direction. Looking down, I would see the trails leading up from base camp and several other groups attempting the climb. Wait! I can get the same type of view much closer and without the annoying cold. I had heard of a race where runners climb the stairs of the Empire State Building. It might as well be a mountain, it stretched so far into the sky. The view would be gorgeous from the top of Manhattan, staring at the rows of perfectly lined streets and avenues. Gorgeous. *I want to climb the Empire State Building.*

I have a logical mind sprinkled with a dusting of obsessive-compulsive disorder and I could not leave The List with only eight items. What else is there? I watched some television, but mostly with a blank stare. The medication limited my ability to focus and reason. Finally, the epiphany for the next item came from merely watching a man in a commercial riding a bicycle. My next thought was the Ironman Triathlon, a purely illogical jump. The Ironman would be an enormous test: 2.4 miles of swimming, 112 miles of biking and 26.2 miles of running. Man, I could never finish that even if I were healthy. The event must take days to complete. I scratched the words on The List. Visiting Hawaii, where they race the Ironman, would be cool. Jennifer would love to go on that trip. Done. We are going to Hawaii! *I want to do the Ironman.*

Swimming was something I was good at growing up. Frankly, I am faster in my mind than I ever was in the pool, but I was good in a small-town sense. My Grandma Jane taught me to swim off her dock at Echo Lake. I was only five and it was the dog paddle at first. She had a cement

seawall bordering her property with two or three steps leading into the lake. The bottom of the lake in front of her house
was green with muck, with leaves fallen from years past accumulated on the bottom. It felt like walking in cold, stewed
spinach. Grandma Jane wore a bathing cap, a pink one with
tiny green plastic flowers. She never liked getting her face
or hair wet, nor did she like stepping in the spinach. She
would go down the steps and gently push off, keeping her
head and toes safe. I learned to swim the same way.

Years later, after developing a decent backstroke in
high school, I would return to the Summer Camp, as we
called my grandparents' home on Echo Lake, to swim for a
week at a time. Late in the afternoon, after my grandfather
had returned from work, I would go out with my grandparents in their steel rowboat. They would sit in the boat while
I remained in the water. I clipped the line of the boat to my
bathing suit and set off swimming the backstroke down the
lake. There was a small island just under a half mile from
their dock, and each night I would tow them around the island. It was peaceful and relaxing for me and certainly
seemed much easier than a Jack LaLanne birthday special.

I enjoyed swimming even though I had given it up.
Training in college was miserable. The pressure to swim
harder and faster made me grow to dislike one of the things
I was good at in my life. But with that era behind me, I now
wanted to swim again. Jennifer swam in high school; maybe
the combination of our genes could make Max or Haley a
good swimmer. We could have our own medley relay. I
wanted to swim again. The List now had nine items. I
needed just one more. The most important one. Each of the
first nine items built to a crescendo, and the finale needed

to be a work of art. Where would I swim? The obvious answer: the English Channel, the hardest swim in the world. That would fit nicely at the apex of The List. But, that swim had been accomplished plenty of times over the past hundred years. No, I wanted to find a swim that was my own. An unprecedented swim. The problem was that I couldn't come up with an unprecedented swim at the moment. Damn. Oh, well. For someone under copious amounts of medication I was making strong progress towards some life goals. I picked up the paper again and completed The List. *I want to complete an unprecedented swim.* The blanks could be filled in later with more perspective than just staring at the tips of motionless toes.

Chapter Seven

The next day, the morning doctor read my chart and rubbed my toes. I could feel his touch and the pressure he applied to my feet. The mental paralysis was passing. I could visualize myself getting out of the bed and eventually walking again. The woman contestant on *The Price is Right* was jumping in the front row as she guessed the price, without going over, of some dining set. The sound of the show was muted and I focused on the gentle squeezing in my toes, my morphine controller nestled next to my right arm. I hadn't medicated today. The nurses had steadily given me other medications throughout the three days I'd been in the hospital, but I didn't use the plunger today.

The doctor made a few more notes and asked me if I wanted to get out of bed and try walking.

"Right now?"

My mind quickly left the Burbank studios and snapped into the present.

"No," he said. "But today. I'll bring some people to help you later this afternoon."

I was ecstatic. I was prepared to cross the number one item off The List. By the end of next week, I should be able to finish The List. I should have made The List harder. Walk? Pshaw. The marathon should be in the first spot to make room for space exploration or something cool like that.

Looking down the middle of the room, I could see myself strutting back and forth through the aisle, occasion- ally bending both elbows like I was in a vaudeville act. Maybe I would entertain the other patients in the room with a small amount of juggling, although I'd better not drop any of the balls because I wasn't sure I could bend over to pick them up. I looked to the floor and could see myself splayed along the cold tiles. Immobile and in pain. Pain and cold. I shivered as if I had walked past a gravestone. I reached for the plunger and self-medicated. I felt the medicine take its effect on me and I closed my eyes.

"Are you ready to walk?" the morning nurse asked.

My nap was interrupted by the morning nurse. I nodded. Nervousness changed my breathing. I steeled my mind for the unknown. Would my legs respond? It was humbling to think that I was going to take my first steps, not unlike a baby. Babies are different. They don't think of the pain involved; they simply want to get up. They have the internal drive to climb up and walk. I needed to give myself that same drive.

The nurse brought Chinzilla with her, and they stood on each side of my bed. The morning nurse gently slid my legs to the left and Chinzilla swiveled my back, but fairly roughly. My feet touched the ground and I smiled with excitement. I instantly felt woozy as I put more weight on my feet, remnants of lying prone for a day. Both nurses positioned themselves under each of my arms. It was go time. My steps were awkward. I envisioned Fred Astaire gliding through the room. I felt like Frankenstein – clumsy, plodding. My feet were barely shuffling. After ten steps, I was exhausted and told the nurse that I'd better lie down. She subtly challenged me by asking if I could walk to the door to see the layout of the hospital wing. The design of the hospital wing was of no interest to me, but her tone implied that I couldn't do it. How was I going to achieve the next nine items on The List if I couldn't walk to the door? My body was heating up. Beads of perspiration broke out on my forehead as I inched closer towards the hallway. Both nurses provided continuous encouragement with each movement forward.

Reaching the doorway left me satisfied and relieved. There was a buzz of nurses and orderlies moving through the hallways. None of them seemed to notice or care that I was able to get out of my bed and walk twelve feet. Yesterday, I prayed my hardest for the ability to walk again and today my prayer was answered. The effects of the morphine vacated my body and the feeling of self-satisfaction filled the void. My legs started to buckle from exhaustion and the nurses caught me.

"Are you ready to go back?"

Damn. Suckered. I had completely lost track of the concept that what goes up must come down. What goes out must come back. The nurses turned me around. I took a deep breath that sent an electric shock up my suture line. Then I shook my head no. I had had enough for today.

"Trent, we're not going to bring in a wheelchair for twelve feet. You can reach the bed."

She was right. The walk back was tiring, but otherwise uneventful.

Later in the afternoon two more nurses helped me walk. This time we went into the hallway. We walked with locked arms, looking like the opening of *The Monkees*. "*Here we come...*" I made it to the nurses' station, the Grand Central of the fifth floor. Even though one of the nurses kept the back of my gown closed as we walked, I felt exposed. I could feel people staring at the stitches on my back under the fly paper. We turned around and walked back to bed at a faster pace. I was getting more comfortable on my new legs.

They released me from the hospital several days later. I reached the point where I could walk down the hallway under the nurse's supervision and without support. I guess that was my final test. Modern medicine is more concerned about infections and malpractice than healing under watchful care.

My house needed to undergo some changes. We lived in a small Cape Cod-style house, which was tiny for our growing family and now was going to need an extra bedroom on the first floor because the second item on The

List was still incomplete -- climbing stairs. We ordered a hospital bed for me to use while I was recuperating. More useful to me than its ability to adjust to twenty positions was the metal handle above the frame from which I could use my good arm to lift myself into the bed. Jennifer and my mother moved the dining room furniture against the walls to provide room for the large bed to be wheeled in and placed in front of the bay window facing the front yard. Such a beautiful concept - a bed that provided me a magnificent view of birds flying past my house, which doubled as a queer sight for neighbors walking past. A bad rendition of Jimmy Stewart's *Rear Window* character prompted Jennifer to find me a little more privacy.

The bed cost nearly $1,500 to rent, an astronomical sum and not covered by any medical insurance. The drugs in my bloodstream had diminished my negotiating and shopping skills so we settled on the first overpriced bed offered to us. The price of that bed invoked a hatred inside me. I felt like a victim again damaged by a different kind of boater.

Jennifer made chicken and stuffing on Wednesdays, one of my favorites in her cooking repertoire. It was a dish that Max would eat, a significant point because that list was very small. Jennifer dutifully served the kids and me everything we needed for dinner. She was a good, short Irish girl. Those are her words, not mine. Ten years earlier, I was selling timeshares in St. Croix for the winter, not exactly a Jack Kerouac adventure, but gorgeous nevertheless. Our relationship was beginning to bloom and I left town because I felt it was getting a little serious for me. Jennifer had planned to visit me in St. Croix during February vacation, about six weeks after I had left. Long-distance calling rates were still robbery, meaning we wrote to each other rather than spend much time on the telephone. To fly from Providence to St. Croix, you needed to connect through Charlotte, San Juan, and St. Thomas, each plane successively smaller and the last looked like it was made in shop class. Jennifer, in her charismatic style, decided that she would "airmail" herself to me. She stepped off the plane and walked down the stairs dressed in a gray plastic sack. It was squared off at the edges and rectangular. Only her head and legs poked through. Her arms were out wide holding the rectangle in place. I laughed hard watching her come off the plane, making her statement and trying to remain composed. The envelope was addressed to me at my condo in Christiansted. She had mailed herself to me! The return address was "Short Irish Girl" with her home address. I don't recall how much postage was required to send her, but I was thrilled that the package arrived safely. My short Irish girl, now clearing the dinner plates and nursing me back to health.

Slow recovery accented by periods of extreme boredom was modus operandi. I tried to focus on The List but struggled just getting out of bed to use the bathroom, located only eight feet away. I watched a cat parade past the front window and thought how many of my nine lives I burned surviving the accident.

Flashbacks came often. Usually, it was the same two scenes repeating over in my head: waving my paddle towards the boat and watching the boat speed away while I probed the gashes in my back. The memories sent pain down my back, real or imagined. My sleep was fitful. I would stir in my sleep and feel like I was being hit with a Taser in my lower back. I would lie awake wondering about the trade-off between being able to walk again and suffering the pain from my surgery. Would I give up the first to rid myself of the second?

My mother stayed with us the first few weeks. She would put me into a recliner after breakfast and hand me the remote. From the number of advertisements on television, one would assume that twenty percent of the population suffered from mesothelioma. There were five of us in the house now. Who wasn't feeling well? It couldn't be me. What more could God do to break me down? Boils...leprosy...mesothelioma? Bruce Springsteen wrote a song in the 1990s, "64 Channels With Nothing On." The Boss nailed that one. I took my OxyContin on schedule, watched crap for six hours, dozed regularly, and waited for the kids to come home. That was my new routine.

Slowly, I prepared myself to reintegrate back to work. The plan was to work at first two hours a day, progressing to a full day. My mother drove me to work on my first Monday back. I reviewed a long list of unread emails, then left my office to attend the weekly staff meeting in the conference room upstairs. On my ride into work that morning, I hadn't yet contemplated negotiating the very steep flight of stairs. I had been able to climb the three stairs to my house and now the three stairs into my office building, but the staircase in front of me appeared mountainous. I held onto the railing, frightened to find out whether I could make the climb. More daunting was the thought of what would happen if I got stuck, or worse, if I fell back down. Would I go back to the hospital? Would I actually paralyze myself this time?

My co-worker, Vin Graziano, met me at the bottom stair. He welcomed me back to work and asked how I was doing. My normal reply to this type of question would have been "I've never felt better in my life!" Today, my fear of the staircase limited me to a mutter.

"Good."

"Can I help you up the stairs?"

I nodded and Vin put his hand gently under my arm. We moved slowly up the staircase. I never looked towards the top. I concentrated solely on each step that was in front of me. After a very long climb we reached the top and I stopped to catch my breath.

"Thank you," I said, barely above a whisper.

We walked down the corridor towards the conference room. Without realizing it, I had checked two items off The List: return to work and climb stairs, in the same morning. It didn't feel momentous or noteworthy. It felt normal.

Now, however, the work seemed less important; it seemed to be a perfunctory component of a day whose only highlights were the smells in the air, taste of my food, and the laughter of my children. Having nearly lost my life had given me a perspective on how to enjoy the little things. I smiled more. I listened more. I made an effort to understand people better, which was a huge improvement from being a spoiled only child. I developed compassion for others. Maybe it had been dormant inside me, awakened by the accident.

I read the *Left Behind* book series about the rapture and the trials of those God called later. I related to their struggles as they tried to find worth and value in their lives knowing they were not pure enough. The characters felt that they were born to a new purpose in the wake of being denied God's call. I was spared. With less than millimeters of difference, I was spared from a wheelchair or death. I was struck by how profound the difference was. Millimeters from needing to develop an entirely different plan for my life. Just millimeters from not being here and feeling this burden. What can I do with my life to repay this magnificent fortune?

Chapter Eight

The boat is following me. I turn to the left then to the right and the boat is right behind me. I scream loudly but no words come out. Why can't they hear me? There is no paddle in my hands to signal to the boat. I wave wildly, extending my fingers as far as they will reach into the sky. The full moon is glowing behind me and my hands cast a shadow onto the placid bay. The boat is moving, up on plane, at a high rate of speed yet somehow it remains at a fixed distance away from me. There is enough distance for them to turn away, to avoid me, but they hold true to their course. The boat keeps coming. The strike is imminent. I brace for impact. My chest pushes forward in the kayak with my arms behind as if I am struggling in bondage. The boat stays on plane bearing down on me.

I need to get out of the kayak. In this position, the boat will hit me in the head and mutilate me, and then the propellers will decapitate me, cutting into my neck with four successive slices. The night air is cool, but my body is sweating. Sweat is pouring down my face and my chest. I can see the propellers spinning in perfect symmetry, each blade silently entering the water forming an evil smile.

I force myself away from the kayak. Get out! Get out! Get out! The water is dark and frightening yet may be my salvation. Get out! I cannot get out of the kayak. The boat stays on plane bearing down on me. In the fraction of a second before I touch the dark water I can hear it fizzing. The water looks different, lighter, as if touched by sun. And, it smells like ginger ale.

"Trent, wake up honey. You're drenched in sweat."

My mother was standing above me.

"Wake up and have a drink," she said.

My eyes were open but not seeing, as if locked in a tomb for years and recently discovered. My mother sat on the couch next to my recliner.

"Have a drink," she said. "The medicine is getting to you."

I smiled what little smile I could muster and scanned the room to make sure that I was not in the bay.

"Thanks," I said in a voice dry and weak. "I'm tired."

My mother handed me a glass of ginger ale.

"Here," she said.

I sipped the ginger ale through the straw in the glass, leaned my head back against the headrest and let the OxyContin continue to poison me. The OxyContin gave me fitful dreams and made me moody. My moodiness could have been because of the accident, as it wasn't my normal demeanor. The medicine's effects on my pain paled in comparison to its effect my mind. I took another sip of ginger ale and closed my eyes. Putting myself in the path of an oncoming motorboat wasn't the first time that I had nearly killed myself. I could vividly see my mother and me standing in front of the mirror watching blood pour down my face. I was drinking ginger ale that night, too.

It had happened one week before the state swimming championships in my senior year of high school. I was madly in love with my high school sweetheart, Paula. On our way to her high school's Valentine's Day mixer, I tried to explain that I was resting my legs for the state championships and that I wouldn't be dancing much that evening. I also tried to explain to her that I needed to be home by 11:00, per Coach's orders. Paula applied the finishing touches to her already-perfect makeup without particularly listening. For a high school squeeze, Paula always knew how to make herself look good. She had chestnut hair, dark eyes and eyebrows, and a creamy olive skin that carried the glow of a tan the year through.

The DJ played Triumph's "Magic Power" and Rose Royce's "Wishing on a Star" at every dance. Our Lady of Fatima High School had used the same DJ for the past several years and that DJ played the exact same songs at the exact same time each dance. At 10:30, "Magic Power" ended and I told Paula that it was time to leave. She pouted because "Wishing on a Star" was still coming. Paula wasn't impressed that I was trying to preserve my legs a week before the state championships or that my coach demanded we all get to bed before 11:00. She was embarrassed to leave before we could dance to the slow, soulful sounds of Rose

Royce for the millionth time, but ultimately she obliged and we headed home.

The snow was falling gently during the ride to bring Paula home. Necking with Paula could often span for days, or so it seemed. Our making out on her doorstep was abbreviated as I steadfastly maintained that I needed to get to bed. Paula again pouted and shut the door sharply as she entered her house. We lived in the same town, only a couple of miles apart. In our early days of dating, I would bike over in less than 10 minutes. Now that I was driving my mom's old Mustang, I could make it home significantly faster, but on that night I took my time as this was my first winter of snow driving. Turning onto Sherry Avenue, Dan Hartmann's "I Can Dream About You" was playing. The speed limit on this road was only 15 mph and I slowed down. Just another Mustang broken in the corral. What was I planning to do tomorrow…maybe…..

Something was different. My vision blurred and there was a ringing in my ears. I could hear someone calling me, tugging at my jacket, but I couldn't comprehend what was happening. The car was stationary and the driver's door was open. I tried to speak, but I had lightning bolts in my throat. I winced from the pain and tried to wipe away the water in my eyes. Directly in front of my face, I could see a hole in the windshield, but only for a second as my eyes filled with stinging water again. The tug on my jacket was more demanding now. I allowed myself to be carried out of the car. A woman, rather a girl, had her arm around me and was trying to steady me on my feet. We walked listlessly up the street as the snow fell like a hard rain. The flakes were cold and searing, pressing into the flesh on my forehead. *I'm wishing on a star, to travel where you are.* The music was pure. It was the song I had missed earlier and now it was playing while she supported my walking up the street. She pushed the doorbell of a house just up the street from where we left the car. Waiting for the door to open, I looked down and noticed that the snow on the front door-step was spotted with red...blood? More and more appeared. I was transfixed by the changing color of the snow.

A middle-aged man opened the door and started speaking with the girl holding me up. I continued to be fascinated by the red designs in the snow. The man led me into the house and a different woman promptly put a towel on my head. The sting resuscitated my senses and I could feel stabbing and gouging in my forehead. The couple led me to the kitchen and seated me at the kitchen table. I was starting to comprehend the situation. I had been in an accident of some kind. I was hurt. I was bleeding. And, I needed to call my mother. I spoke my telephone number and they dialed for me. My mother picked up on the first ring and I told her what happened, then I handed the phone back to the man and asked him to tell my mom where I was. It turned out that I was less than a half-mile away from my house. Within seconds, my mother came rushing in the front door and without any emotion she took control of the scene like a *M.A.S.H.* triage nurse. She whisked me to the bathroom to clean me. Standing in front of the bathroom mirror, my mother started to wipe some of the blood away from my forehead but stopped. She let me bleed for a minute.

"Take a good look at yourself, Trent," she said. "Take a good look at what you did to yourself."

I looked intently into the mirror. I was wearing a red parachute parka that matched the blood flowing from my scalp. I could see the skin cut open in my scalp and the blood seeping out towards my eyes. My eyebrows failed in trying to channel the blood away from my eyes. Blood caked around the corners of my eyes, crusting with each blink. My cheeks were red from the chill of the February air, the capillaries flushed from cold and excitement. Blood funneled toward my chin and flowed into the sink basin. My face had the same quality as Martin Sheen's in *Apocalypse Now*. I would always remember this face.

The rescue workers had arrived and directed me back to the kitchen where they could care for me properly. They stanched the bleeding as best they could without giving me stitches. They were concerned because my head had been lacerated by the windshield glass and many of the tiny fragments were still embedded in my skin.

"Were you drinking tonight, son?" one of them asked.

I shook my head.

"Are you sure you weren't drinking?"

Again, I shook my head. My throat was throbbing and I did not want to speak out of fear of being struck by lightning again.

"Son, it's important that you tell me what you were drinking to know the medicines to give you."

"Ginger ale," I mouthed, unable to get the words out. When I tried again I was able to eke out the words, but my voice sounded foreign, guttural, and I had to grab my throat because of the pain.

I woke up in tears. I had nearly killed myself again. Now, as I recovered ever so slowly from being run over by a boat, I had to wonder: by what grace of God was I able to survive two accidents like this? It must have been torture for my mother to watch this scene again. She prayed the night of my car accident and she prayed again the night of my boating accident. She told me, when I was younger, that I had a guardian angel. Her father, my grandfather, had died two days after I was born. She told me that he fought to stay alive long enough to see me. Maybe he was my guardian angel? If so, he had done a stellar job.

Chapter Nine

Is there a soundtrack for rehab?

Maybe it's some over-produced Celine Dion ballad that drones on and on? That's what electrical stimulation feels like, a Celine Dion song that hits you unexpectedly with a bolt of lightning to the weakest part of your body. Three days a week. I returned to the therapist diligently because I wanted to walk normally again -- not because of The List. The List was the furthest thing from my mind as the therapist, Steve Mignacca, worked to break up the scar tissue. Steve was an old friend. In our twenties, we had played hours of basketball at a time, with endless energy, the way twenty-year-olds do. Steve was quite different in the therapy office. He was caring and concerned about how I felt. The Steve I knew back in the day didn't give a rat's ass how I was feeling. My having an epileptic seizure would have meant an undefended layup. Here, he was compassionate even while using his strong hands to break apart the tissue.

The first thing he did at every visit was apply heat to my back. I would lie on the trainer's table with a steaming two-pound pack on my back. The warming process took around five minutes. Then, Steve would apply the electric pads to my back and turn on the stimulation machine. This therapy took ten to twelve minutes. I would lie there and wait. Physical therapy gives one too much time to think. The mind should be thinking about how the body is getting stronger. Unfortunately, the solitude of physical therapy leads the mind to think about the obstacles one faces and the physical challenges it takes to overcome those obstacles. I would lie on the bench with the heat and the stim applied to my back and sulk in a morose mood, thinking that I would never be strong again, knowing that this perfunctory effort was meaningless. I felt this same despair when I was younger.

I was in my senior year of college and, by then, had tired of swimming. I had plateaued. It was time to make life decisions and I wasn't the right guy to handle mine. My parents had left Rhode Island for a better job in the Midwest a year earlier, I was going through the motions with the girl I was dating, I wasn't attending classes, and the darkness of winter was approaching. I was depressed.

Standing in my pantry cleaning the sink, I thought, *I hate washing dishes. Why bother?* Living with three college guys is like hogs milling around in their own feces. Nothing gets cleaned. Nothing gets put away. Everything gets left behind or pushed around. And why did I care? I was twenty and going nowhere -- except to my job as a dishwasher or waiter somewhere.

I stared out the pantry window and saw myself in the reflection. I needed a goal, a purpose, a reason. But me and the guy in the window reflection both knew we weren't goal-setters. So, I made a resolution. I resolved to try hard in practice the next day. I resolved to move up one lane and leave it in the pool each and every set. Even if I couldn't make a life goal, or a relationship goal, or a career goal, surely I could make a simple commitment to working hard for one day.

The next day, I honored my promise and left practice exhausted. Then I made myself one more promise – come back tomorrow. I would come back again and knock myself out. Every day it was the same for the two weeks leading to our first dual meet against the University of Maine. The bus ride to Maine was long and boring. I sat in my seat, looked out the window, and realized how much I hated racing. I hated the pomp and circumstance of racing. I hated the dread of racing. I hated seeing the results of racing. Swimming is a sport about the clock and little about competition. Boxing is competition. Boxing is personal. Beating a guy senseless leaves a clear winner and a clear loser. Swimming was just an event and with the exception of swimming against Boston College there was very little to get excited about.

My team warmed up together with a small set, then broke up to practice starts and turns. I went to the deep end to practice backstroke turns. Each pool is a little different for backstrokers. Freestylers simply followed the thin black line at the bottom, but backstrokers needed to adjust to the height of the ceiling and travel without looking at the coming turn. The University of Maine pool was 25 yards long, which meant that the backstroke flags were five yards from the end. Standard distance. I practiced a few turns at half speed to acclimate to the ceiling, then started on my full speed turns. During the first full speed turn, I planted my hand against the wall, but it slipped and I felt a pull deep in my shoulder. Athletes learn early in their careers the difference between being hurt and being injured. What I had just felt was my first experience with the latter.

I exited the pool quickly, toweled off, put on my warm-ups, and went to the concrete wall behind our team bench and started to stretch. The soreness was wrong. The shoulder didn't respond with a sigh of relief as it did the thousand other times I used that series of stretches. The pain was deeper. My muscle was begging me to stop, quit, cease! My eyes teared. The 400-medley relay was the first event of college dual meets and the backstroke leg was the first of the relay. I was twenty minutes removed from my new injury and two hundred miles removed from where I wanted to be. I hated racing. I gave our team a lackluster performance and lost to the Maine backstroker by a good margin. I sat in the stands by myself and moped. I told Coach O'Neill that my shoulder was tight and that I wanted to scratch the 200-meter individual medley. He obliged. Now, I was alone in the stands and would be for the next hour and a half until the 200-metter backstroke. I put on my headphones and listened to a cassette of classic rock I had borrowed from a teammate. During the layover, I heard "Ain't Seen Nothing Yet" by The Who. (I know now that the band was Bachman Turner Overdrive – but it sounded like The

Who the first time I listened.) I heard "All Right Now" by Free and "White Room" by Cream. The music was awesome, but it failed to motivate me and they were swimming the 500-yard freestyle, the event before the 200-yard back-stroke. I got up and tried to stretch my shoulder. No good. *Shit*, I thought, *I can't believe this is happening to me.* I'm not typically a sore loser, but I was pissed. I had just finished the hardest two weeks of practice of my life and my reward for setting the goal was to injure my shoulder on a practice turn.

I walked behind my block and watched the end of the 500-yard freestyle. The swimmer from Maine in the middle lane won the race, got out of the pool, and stood behind his block. No way! It was the same kid who had beaten me in the medley relay, and now he was looking to go double with the 500-free and 200-back. My lifelong friend, Dave Hardy, was getting ready to swim on the other side of this prick. Dave leaned over toward me.

"This guy just told me that he's going to kick your ass," Dave said.

"He ain't seen nothin' yet," I said, glaring at Dave and my opponent.

Baby, you ain't seen nothin' yet. I jumped in the pool, went through my normal pre-race routine and looked at the kid next to me. *I'll give you something you'll never forget.* The race started and I took immediate control. At the 100-yard turn, I had a body length lead on the Maine swimmer. Perhaps the strongest part of my backstroke was my turns. The earlier issue aside, I had perfected the Naber spin turn, which helped me compensate for my lack of speed. During the race, I hit the 100-yard turn, spun, but waited a beat at the wall underwater. I waited for the Maine swimmer to turn and get into my equal position. I stared at him under the water, I flashed him a quick smile and a wave of my hand. *You ain't seen nothing yet, prick.* And I proceeded to smoke him over the next 100 yards.

Coach O'Neill stopped me on my way to get my sweats.

"Nice race," he said.

Coach was never a verbose man. I looked at his watch. It was my fastest 200 backstroke time in two years. Nice race? That wasn't a race. That was personal. I went back to the bench and sat alone with the throbbing in my shoulder, not sure whether I would go to practice tomorrow.

The timer went off on the stim machine and brought me back to the physical therapy room. Steve removed the leads and the heat and started to rub into my scar tissue. The massage was like having a stone in your shoe forcing you to step awkwardly to avoid direct pain.

After exercising my back, Steve gave me my weekly list of homework assignments. He photocopied several pages of pictures of people doing stretches with numbers next to them like "3x" or "5x" to represent the number of repetitions he wanted for each. The primary series of stretches made me look like a supplicant kneeling and praying to Allah. Steve corrected me on how I should be doing the stretches better. He said he wanted my back to be like an elastic band, able to stretch out and easily return to its original shape. Unfortunately, my back was more like a lead pipe. No flexibility yet, but very useful to Colonel Mustard in the Lounge.

My shoulder never fully recovered from the tear in college. I never regained full use and I wondered if the same would happen to my back. What limits would there be on my being normal? The day's session improved my body. Although the winter was coming and I could feel the cold affecting the tightness of the muscles in my back, I was getting less protective of the injured area. I felt more comfortable walking through my office, but I was still nervous walking in crowds, fearing that someone would touch my back and send me back to the hospital bed.

Chapter Ten

The accident did not lower the levels of testosterone in my body for long. Soon, I started waking up at attention regularly. My mind started to shift to scratching number five off The List: sex with my wife. This was normally a challenge in itself with two small children, working two jobs, a grape pickers' strike in Napa Valley, and a host of other convenient excuses. Determination settled in and I started to make my move one Saturday night over a pitcher of margaritas.

"No," she said.

A familiar refrain. I went through the repertoire of my not-so-cool moves, but to no avail.

"Please," I asked sweetly. "We haven't had sex in a really long time."

"Trent, it's not that I don't want to have sex. It's…it's that I'm afraid I'm going to break you."

I'm glad she thought one of us was a rodeo bull in bed.

"You won't break me. I'll be okay."

The tone in my voice turned from sweet to desperate, not too far removed from every boy late on a Saturday night.

"T, I want you to get your doctor's permission first."

Permission? I need permission to have sex? Mother, may I? Er….really bad image.

"My next doctor's appointment isn't for three weeks."

"We can wait."

We?! Maybe you, but this case of cat scratch fever is burning my blood. I guess I could call the doctor and move up the appointment. I would have to wait until Monday to do that. No good. Wait, I could call 911 right now. The ambulance could pick me up, chauffeur me to the emergency room, I would work out a deal with the doctor and be back in the sack in a few hours. My deductible was met this year. I might want to put some pants on before calling. Man, this sucks. Permission for sex? "Doctor," the triage nurse said trying not to laugh loudly, "the patient is here tonight complaining of permission for sex."

"Good night," she said.

Life with small children moved forward wonderfully as it always does, with breakfasts and baths, snuggling and stories. Three weeks passed and I was in my doctor's examination room having my scar tissue prodded and squeezed. The muscles on the left side of my back were in a constant spasm, causing me to lean to the left, looking like I was perpetually in the middle of an "I'm A Little Teapot" song. The doctor told me that the cold weather would be bad for my muscles until they healed to the point of maximum improvement and I should expect the lean. He reminded me that they had pared away inches of muscle on each side of the wound to eliminate the potential for infection. The lean was a small price to pay for no bacteria. Yup, whatever you say, doc. You're not the one walking like you're eighty years old.

The examination ended and I started to get dressed when the doctor asked if I had any questions. There was only one on my mind. It's the only question I'd had on my mind for the past three weeks, or the last twenty years if you put a different lens on it.

"Can I have sex?" I asked.

"Well, the accident shouldn't have caused any damage to your reproductive system. There may be some muscular discomfort which…"

"That's not what I meant. My wife is afraid that she's going to break me. I have to get permission from you to have sex."

The doctor nodded while rubbing the back of his neck, stood up, walked to his desk and started writing. He returned with a piece of paper that is now arguably the most monumental document in American history since the Declaration of Independence. A prescription from his pad read, 'Trent is cleared for **ALL** activities.' Game on! I wanted to click my heels like Fred Astaire, but it probably would have come off more like Fred Flintstone, so I decided just to thank my doctor and be on my way.

There aren't many sure things in life. That night, sex was a sure thing. The doctor said so! I went to work waiving my prescription as if it was a winning Powerball ticket. My excitement was brimming and I left a little early, thinking that if I played my cards right, we could have some action before we picked the kids up from childcare, then a little more later that night.

I bounded through the door and proudly displayed my prescription.

"Call your mother and ask her to pick up the kids. And let's go upstairs." I was already marching to my own John Philip Sousa beat, headed towards the staircase.

"I've already got dinner cooking. You should have told me that you were coming home early. You could have picked up the kids."

"I didn't want to pick up the kids. I have a prescription. Here, read it. It reads that Trent is cleared for all activities. Notice that all is underlined. Three times!"

I regained my marching beat.

"We can wait until tonight. After we put the kids to bed."

My level of exasperation bordered on apoplectic. A facial tic began to develop along the left side of my mouth.

"I've waited. I waited the three weeks to get to the doctors. I waited three months to heal. And, I waited I don't remember how long before the accident because WE'RE MARRIED WITH TWO KIDS!"

Jennifer stirred the dinner and gave me a coy smile. I knew that smile. I knew what was coming and I began marching again. Jennifer called her mother and made the request. I marched my way towards the stairs, undoing my tie and kicking off my shoes. The smile couldn't be beaten off my face. I had the winning ticket! I looked out the window towards Allin's Cove, where I had put my kayak into the water three months ago. There was a small amount of snow on the ground and along the shoreline. Darkness was setting in early following the winter solstice. The cold sunset was serene. A couple of birds hovered near the water, as if it was too cold for a bath.

"I didn't know you could use dill."

I could hear Jennifer's voice from the kitchen. She was still speaking on the phone with her mother and seemed to be discussing cooking ideas.

"That sounds good. What temperature do you cook it?"

She was talking about food. What the freak is going on here? Jennifer smiled at me and gave me the finger. The good one. The one that means one more minute, but after nine years of marriage I've come to learn that it actually means around eighteen to twenty minutes. My dill was about to pop and this drivel about some roast was irritating me. Frustrated, I gave Jennifer the marching pantomime, foolishly thinking that it would motivate her to stop the conversation. Jennifer shot me a quick look and gave me the good finger again. That meant thirty-seven minutes.

"For everything that is holy in this world, tell your mother that if she wants more grandchildren she will put down the phone right now!" I said, in a much too loud indoor voice.

"I've got to go, Mom."

Jennifer glared at me.

Not exactly the ambiance I was looking to set, but she acquiesced. I never would have guessed that it was easier to climb up a flight of stairs following my paralysis than it was to climb up with Jennifer to scratch number five off The List. On the way up the stairs, I told myself, 'Trent, you better enjoy this because it'll be Easter before you get this shot again.' We closed the bedroom door and I cashed my ticket.

Chapter Eleven

On a Saturday about four months after the accident, I decided that I wanted to do something I often used to do with the kids – take them swimming. These were always special days for me because I had time to bond with them and share my love of the water. According to my doctor, the wounds had healed to the point where I could submerge them in a pool or bath. The risk of infection had passed. My physical play with the children had been limited, mainly now because I harbored residual fears of being reinjured. I still walked with my back turned towards a wall. In crowds, I moved aside so that everyone could pass me and not be behind me. The children didn't know my limits. Swimming would be a nice way to play physically without much stress on my back.

Haley, who is a natural-born fish, was surprisingly reluctant to go. Without an explanation, she simply retreated to her room. Later in the day, Jennifer took her to the market and tried to find out what was wrong, a common trick she would use with Haley. Returning, Jennifer told me that Haley didn't want to see me with my shirt off. She said that she was scared of my scars and they were giving her bad dreams.

I sat down. My soul fell to the floor. My daughter thought I was Frankenstein, a mutilated monster. I was devastated. In the months since the accident, I had spent significant effort and strength healing my body without enough consideration of how my children were managing with the stresses of an injured parent. Haley was scared to see my scars.

Ever the optimist, Jennifer took the issue and turned the concern on its head. The next day, Jennifer asked Max if he knew that Daddy had stripes like a zebra. The imagination of a three-year-old is a magical thing. I could see Max trying to process or reconcile the notion that Daddy was akin to a zebra. He looked at me but didn't know what to say in response.

"Do you want to see Daddy's stripes?" she asked.

Max smiled and nodded.

"Okay, you can see, but you can't touch. They're *owies*."

With that, Jennifer had me kneel down and lift off my shirt. She traced the outline of my scars.

"See Max, just like a zebra."

He smiled a little more and tried to touch the still-tender wounds.

"No, no. We can't touch, we can only look right now. Doesn't Daddy look like a zebra?"

Max was now laughing and started calling me a zebra. Then Jennifer grabbed some of the scant hair on my back.

"Or, maybe he's a hairy monkey? What do you say, Max? Is Daddy a zebra monkey?"

Haley was conspicuously perched on the stairs, watching this interaction through the stair balusters. After a few minutes, she couldn't contain herself, bounded down the stairs, and joined in the zebra-monkey chants. More than the OxyContin and the Celebrex, laughter eased the pain I felt. The joy of my family made me feel that my scars were fading. The love we shared in that room was healing me. I am certain that it is cliché to say that near-death experiences make one appreciate life more. But, it's true. It's all true.

Chapter Twelve

Nearly nine months had passed since the ac-cident. Nine months of longing to do many of the physical activities I had done all my life. I longed to wash away the past nine months of pain and agony, of stretching and of healing. Nine months of being an empty shell of the man I was before. Physical therapy several times per week had me up, moving, and regaining some of the strength in my muscles. I had built up enough strength to run around the block, but in truth, I hated running. There aren't many more boring tasks than to run from one point to another or worse, back to where you started from. Growing up, I was always of the mindset that if you are not running after a ball then why bother. It was a cold June morning when I decided to go to the Newman YMCA in nearby Seekonk, Massachusetts, to join in the Saturday morning pickup basketball game. I had been playing basketball at the YMCA for nearly fifteen years. Moreover, in those fifteen years, I had developed into a respectable low-post player. My ass was large enough to create space to get off any shot, provided that my opponent was no taller than 6' 5". However, the term "respectable" was in the eye of the beholder. The talent at the YMCA pickup games ranged from former Division II College players to men who had difficulties tying their shoes. The twenty or so guys at the gym had been playing against each other, beating each other up, and trash talking each other for decades. Over the years, the games became less about the score and more about the abuse you could administer both physically and verbally. Some say that baseball is the richest sport because of its numerous "unwritten" rules. Baseball is a pauper compared to the unwritten rules created by a group of gray, broken-down, middle-aged men. Gems like, 'play two and you sit,' 'you get the next jump ball,' and 'if you want the ball on offense you need to work on defense.' But also the more personal ones like 'you can't drive to the basket on Frank because he doesn't play defense inside the free throw line,' or 'Jamie rebounds like he's 6'10" because of the extra push he gives you in the back,' or the granddaddy 'you can't call traveling on a man's move.' My 'move' included a double drop step, which may be legal in the travel-crazy NBA, but is certainly illegal to anyone familiar with the actual rules of basketball. Carl traveled nearly every time he moved to the basket. He picked up his pivot foot to gain a quickness advantage. Bob needed a bus transfer to cover his travel fees in the lane. He was famous for pretending to shoot, then making a circle over his head with the ball while taking two steps toward the basket before dribbling. Bob's move couldn't be called a ball fake because he couldn't act that well. The average spectator might think Bob was practicing synchronized swimming moves, but to the guys in the Saturday morning pickup game it was the same move which hadn't fooled anyone for the past fifteen years.

I looked through the doors of the gym and watched some of the players warming up, shooting baskets, taking layups, talking loudly, and pretending to stretch. Part of me felt like an outsider. For the past six months, I had lived only in my house, going Jack Torrance from *The Shining* stir-crazy. I missed the camaraderie and the ball-busting. That, plus I had left the house before Jennifer woke up to object.

Some of the players noticed me immediately and stopped their dribbling and shooting. Then, in one of the most heartwarming moments of my life, all the basketball players stopped what they were doing and started to applaud me. I sheepishly waved them away as I walked to the bench to lace up my sneakers, but they continued to clap and they started to cheer. The applause filled me with a strength that I could never have achieved with years in a weight room. Men who I've sweated on, pushed against, cursed at, humiliated, played foil to, competed with and against, came to me and genuinely hugged and touched me. The glow in my chest was radiating. Then the trash talking continued as if I was never away.

"Did your surgery give you a new right hand? Because your last one sucked."

Perfect. That's what I missed.

We made up teams with the usual arguing about who was trying to stack theirs. Our team was made up of 'big and stupid' which was better than our opponents 'slow and ugly.' The game got underway with a check ball and our team on defense. I requested to play Mike, because he didn't run around so much. Normally, I would have played one of the bigger guys and slapped bodies with him. In my fragile state, I was looking for an opponent who was two dribbles away from a ruptured Achilles.

The ball moved to me on our first possession and I promptly kicked it back to another teammate only to have him return the pass to me. My teammates encouraged me to shoot, which I should add I would never hear again in my life. I took one dribble inside the 3-point line and shot. The ball bounced off the front rim, bounced off the backboard and into the net. Not exactly the shooting from the Jordan/Bird Big Mac challenge, but successful nevertheless. The players, my friends, stopped again and gave me a cheer. I stood at the top of the key and smiled. Perhaps I can recover from this injury. Maybe I can be what I was before. Maybe I can find sports fulfilling again.

"You can sign autographs back on defense," Carl said as he chipped my shoulder going by me.

Chapter Thirteen

In my entire life, I had never had a worse twelve months. It had taken a toll on me both physically and emotionally. I looked in the mirror and saw a man who had aged and a man whose body was different. It was a year of growing wider, rounder, and softer as I convalesced. My appetite had always been healthy and, thankfully, sports provided a modicum of weight control. The layoff of athletic activity didn't diminish my appetite and, in turn, I increased in size. I was still able to see my toes on the one-year anniversary of my accident as I stepped on the scale, but just barely. The last time I was this nervous to step on a scale was for my football weigh-in when I was a youngster.

For one season when I was ten years old I played Pop Warner Football. The week before the start of the season, the team traveled to the neighboring town of Barrington for a weigh-in. This form of pre-pubescent humiliation was an annual ritual for players and coaches alike.

At Barrington High School, we filed off the bus and into the cafeteria. Coach Perry instructed us that our team would weigh in next. He said that the smaller kids only need to take off their shoes. However, the kids who might be closer to the 120-pound weight limit might need to strip down to their skivvies. The heavier kids, he suggested, might want to try to go to the bathroom again. I knew I was one of the heavier kids, but I had gone to the bathroom before I left home. I took off my shirt and my shoes, but I was a little uncomfortable taking my pants off in front of the other fifty kids. There were a dozen other kids already down to their underwear and roughhousing in line. I didn't feel like roughhousing in line. I felt like leaving. Coach Rego walked over and pinched a handful of my belly fat.

"Jesus, Trent! What have you been eating?"

"My dad brought home coffee rolls this morning," I replied.

"Are you kidding me? On the one day you need to make weight you're eating coffee rolls!" Coach Rego howled and consequently a large portion of the team laughed along.

Shirtless, I started laughing and my belly rolls jiggled right along.

It was my turn and I stepped onto the scale shirtless and shoeless, but trousers still intact. After balancing, the scale rested at 122 pounds, three pounds over. The referee suggested that my pants and socks might be worth a few pounds. I disrobed while everyone watched. It seemed like everyone in the school filtered into the room to watch the greatest weigh-in since Ali-Frazier III. The pants and socks only shaved a measly one pound off the total. Coach Perry told me that they would reweigh me within one hour.

"Trent," he said, "it's very simple. If you want to play football, you need to lose two pounds in the next hour."

I was near tears. I was shaking in the corner of the cafeteria, holding my clothes in front of my fat body.

"I don't know how to lose two pounds!"

Coach Perry got down on one knee and looked me in the eye.

"You need to run. There is a track behind the school. You need to go onto the track and run as hard as you can for as long as you can. It's very simple."

I hated running.

"You go out there and start running and don't stop until I come and get you. I'll be out in a little while."

I really hated running. Running is fine if you're trying to stretch a single into a double or if you're playing a good game of manhunt, but I couldn't imagine a time where I would just go out and run because I had nothing better to do.

As advertised, the track was right behind the school. The large oval with painted lines seemed like a stupid place to run. Who wanted to run in circles? Couldn't we just run to the street corner and back? I started trotting on the track. I started first putting yards behind me, then tenths of miles, then quarter miles. The running was exhausting and Coach Perry took a long time to come and get me. This running was starting to feel suspiciously like the 'who can stay quiet the longest game' my parents played with me in the car. I kept running around the lines. Sometimes I would make my legs cross the lines and other times I would pretend that they were a force field, which would electrocute me if I crossed.

There were other chubby kids at the track, too. Other boys who probably didn't eat a coffee roll that morning, but had just grown a little too fast. Some of the boys would leave and new ones who failed the weigh-in would replace them. Coach Perry yelled for me to come and see him. They were ready for me. At the scale, my legs were throbbing and sweat was pouring down my body like a leaky faucet.

"Did you run the whole time?"

"Yes, sir. I went around the track fifteen times."

"Fifteen times? That's almost four miles. Are you sure that's how many laps you did?"

"Yes, sir. I count everything."

We entered the building and I made a beeline to the water bubbler. Coach Perry smacked me in the back of my head.

"Trent, you just ran to lose weight and now you're running to gain it right back at the bubbler? Are you a moron?"

"No, sir," I answered.

"No, you're not." He laughed. "Now go back into the cafeteria, take off your clothes, and get back on the scale."

This time the scale registered 119 pounds and the referee approved me for Pee Wee football. I apologized for sweating all over his scale and promptly got dressed.

I stepped on the scale now, twenty-five years later, and it registered 218 pounds, 100 pounds heavier than Pee

Wee football. I could have eaten Haley, Max, and a box of Twinkies and not gained 100 pounds. The scale remained the same as I stood on it for a minute longer. A year ago, I was 20 pounds lighter.

The one-year anniversary did come with a small present: I was able to move forward on The List. In hindsight, the first six were easy: walk, climb a flight of stairs, lift my children, return to work, go to a Red Sox game, and make love to Jennifer. Now it was time to push myself to see if I was healed in the body as well as the mind. It was time to train.

Chapter Fourteen

The beginning of year two did not start with a boxing bell ringing and a Rocky Balboa montage. I honestly thought it might, and was disappointed that I could only run around the block once before being winded. Late September and early October's cool mornings greeted me each day as I tried to exercise before work. In basketball, it was becoming easier for me to compete and stay with the average athletes. The ounces and pounds were beginning to trickle off.

I went to the Barrington YMCA for my first swimming workout in over ten years. Thankfully, Jennifer had the decency to buy me a swimsuit in which I would not be compared to a beluga whale or one of the 'pickle' suits I would have worn in my college swimming days.

Unlike the old days, I eased myself into the water rather than diving. Post-traumatic stress disorder was a topic on the lips of many media outlets as soldiers were returning from Afghanistan. My mind had suffered plenty of setbacks over the past year. My hands had turned numb as I was driving on the highway, behind a boat on a trailer, staring at its massive propeller. The sounds of buoy markers sent chills through my lower extremities. I could hear them after I had surfaced from the accident, I could hear them as I drove around town, and I could hear them in my head as I lay down to sleep. Fortunately, I did not have any issues with climbing into the water. Thank goodness for small miracles.

There was no power in my swimming stroke. I was moving only slightly better than the geriatrics who walked along the slow lane. The things I could do for hours on end now felt like hours to the end. I plodded along, following the black line in lane three as my mind drifted to the first time I had swum in this pool.

Is there a defining moment in everyone's lives when the course of your future is charted? Meeting your spouse? Graduating college? Dropping acid for the first time? For me, I was twelve years old at J.N. Webster Boy Scout Camp with Troop 6 from Bristol for our annual weeklong semi-camping trip. Without knowing it at the time, the trip paved the path for nearly every relationship I have had since.

I was working on my lifesaving merit badge that year. Midway through the week, as we broke camp, my Scoutmaster John Greene suggested that I try the mile swim, which took place on the last morning of the week. He watched me swim for a few days and said that I had talent.

Plus, I would be the only member of the troop to earn the One Mile Swim badge, which I could wear on my uniform. The badge was large and white with a red seahorse insignia. I was constantly looking for ways to stand out in the crowd, and a special badge would more than do the trick. I asked Mr. Greene how far a mile was. He was unsure and walked me over to the lakefront to find out.

The head lifeguard was sitting in his high white chair and looked like a member of KISS without the makeup. Styx's "Blue Collar Man" was blaring on his radio as he started to describe the swim. He said that I needed to swim from the deep water to the far buoy eight times and that I would need a boat to guide me.

"It's a mile just to reach the buoy!" I said. "How do I get ready for that swim in two days?"

"I guess you should swim a few laps in the deep end," Mr. Greene said.

I swam a lap here and there over the next few days, not clear how far I was swimming. I was pretending to train rather than actually training. What did I know? I never swam more than the length of a 25-yard pool at a time.

It was hot at dawn on that Saturday morning and a swim would be a great way to spend the morning. As a bonus, because I had entered into the swim, Mr. Greene excused me from the tasks of cleaning up the campsite. I wished there had been more swim events that could have excused me from work.

Eight people entered the swim. All of them were between fifteen and seventeen years old. I was by far the youngest. A canoe would spot each swimmer.

"To make sure you don't drown," Gene Simmons said.

Gulp!

"How many people drown in this swim?"

"Nearly half," Gene replied.

Gulp! All of a sudden cleaning the campsite sounded like a good idea. We started from the docks and I slogged toward the first buoy. At the first turn, I asked my spotter, Alan Sinclair, how I was doing.

"I thought you were a fast swimmer," he said. "These other kids are killing you."

I was confused.

"I thought the mile was a distance event and I should take it easy."

"Nah," Alan said. "You should swim fast and beat these guys."

So I did. I put my head down and motored back towards the beach, passing four swimmers. I kept the pace going and soon lapped two of the other swimmers. I had more than a full-length lead on the closest swimmer when I got out of the water. I dried off, put on my T-shirt and shoes, then walked down the beach toward the camp jamboree in the central square. One of the J.N. Webster scoutmasters stopped me at the end of the beach as I was walking.

"Did you stop early, son?"

"No, sir."

"You know the mile swim is eight laps?"

"Yes, sir."

"Did you do all eight laps?"

"Yes, he did," said Alan, now standing behind me. "He was the first finisher."

"Good job, young man."

Score one for the chubby kid!

Something happened to me on the way to meet my fellow scouts at the jamboree as I went from having a swagger in my step to a limp. I didn't step on anything or hurt myself, but something inside of me wanted to tell the members of Troop 6 how hard the swim was. How painful it was. How I fought through life and death and freshwater sharks to complete the swim. I was embarrassed to tell them just how easy the swim was.

I guess I feared that if everyone else thought the swim was easy, then they would all try it and everyone would come home with the special badge. It's silly how vanity clouds accomplishments.

When my parents picked me up at the end of the trip home, Mr. Greene told them of my success in the swim and suggested that they should explore putting me on a swim team at the YMCA.

Now I was at the YMCA for my first swim since the accident. The training swim was over to no fanfare or special badges. I pulled for a few hundred yards, I kicked for a while, and swam some backstroke. I didn't attempt any flip turns. I wasn't ready for advanced swimming just yet. During my swim, one set of geriatrics was replaced by another. I left the pool exhausted and in a satisfied mood. I was back in the water. For the first time in a year. Heck, for the first time in fifteen years I was glad to be back in the water.

Chapter Fifteen

Running and I have never been on the best of terms. I've been a dispassionate lover and she's been a complete bitch. I'm pigeon-toed and have stubby legs, not conducive to running. My close friend and college teammate Jay Holbrook ran the Bay State Marathon 10 years ago when he was in his mid-twenties. As an athletic rival, I thought that I should do the same and proceeded to go out for a run to see how it felt. I left my home in Providence and meandered through the perpendicular streets of the Mount Pleasant neighborhood, enjoying the crisp fall air. The only running I had been doing at the time was in my YMCA pickup basketball games and the way we played didn't require a great level of fitness.

After what felt like a reasonable distance, I turned and made my way back to the house. Neighbors could hear my labored breathing as I walked the final street back to my driveway. At the house, I grabbed my car keys and proceeded to drive the route I had just run, to measure the distance of my valiant effort. I couldn't believe the odometer. Just 1.2 miles? That's it? I'm exhausted and I only ran 1.2 miles? My suspicions were confirmed. Running sucked.

Determined to progress on The List, I began to run more. My first few runs following the one-year anniversary had a greater level of suckitude than a decade earlier. Sure, plenty of years had passed and I was now in my mid-thirties, but the bigger handicap was probably the extra twenty pounds I was carrying. Squeezing the rolls around my waist, I thought, *This fat needs to go.*

Over the next three winter months, I attempted to run twice a week. Each run was never more than 2.5 miles. If I tried to go any longer, my back would tire and I would pay for it. I'd have trouble moving the next day at work. On March 1, 2004, I decided that I would attempt to run a 5k. I hadn't tried to run that far in six years.

That was in 1998 and we had just moved to Barrington. Jennifer was looking for ways to involve us in the community and meet folks. She had read an advertisement for a local 5k and thought that it would be a good way for me to find some new friends and get a little exercise. I had never run a road race before, outside of the last part of a couple of sprint triathlons in my late teens. After being cut from the baseball team my senior year in high school, I thought that I might try out for the track team. The running I did in my youth was either out of necessity to evade a group of thugs trying to beat me up or playing manhunt with my Boy Scout troop. I was about to end my high school years and I thought I might expand my horizons. I went to the first meeting of the track team where the coach was giving instructions.

"Okay, guys. We're going on a quick seven-miler down to the State House and back."

What? I thought we'd warm up with a jaunt to the corner candy store and back. Don't I need to do some stretching first?

"Is there a field part of our track and field team?" I asked.

He told me to go grab a discus or javelin and I could start throwing behind the school. Throwing a javelin was going to be awesome because it was like pitching without worrying about hitting the strike zone. That turned out not to be entirely true. In practice on a cold March afternoon, I threw the javelin well outside the target area and nearly speared the field coach who was looking the other way. Coach pulled the javelin out of the ground and marched towards me at double time.

"Did you almost hit me with this javelin?" he asked.

I nodded with my eyes cast downward.

"I want you to give me five laps. Maybe that will help you learn how to throw inbounds!"

I turned around and started doing what I joined the field team to avoid - running.

Sitting at our kitchen table, I thought about Jennifer's plan to introduce me to the neighborhood. When I spoke, my words came out as a whimper.

"I don't think I'm in shape to run a road race."

"You play basketball three times a week," Jennifer replied. "I'm sure that you can finish a little run through town. Besides, you don't have to race. You can take it easy and talk to people along the way."

My wife should know better. If I walk into a men's room and another guy walks in and we start urinating at the same time, it's a race. Period. There is no "talking to people along the way."

The weather on race day was pleasant and drew about 150 people. The event organizer gave a quick speech about the charity, during which I eyeballed the crowd for the real runners. I could see them huddled up stretching each other, about ten of them. From the start, I followed just behind the lead pack. The first mile was slightly uphill towards the country club and the real runners were running in a tight formation like a swarm of gnats around a porch light. The mile marker was just before a right turn and a volunteer shouted out the time. I crossed in 5:50, perfect just like the days of my youth. I was running free and easy and still had plenty of gas in the tank. After the right turn, the second mile started with an even longer uphill climb. I tried to stay with the lead group but they seemed to be picking up the pace on the climb. I worked a little harder to keep in their draft, but this damn hill was steep, at least on the section where I was running.

The mile-two volunteer barked out times as runners passed. 12:25…12:30…12:35…I passed and tried to give a smile but the hill took all the joy out of me. I ran the second mile in 6:45. If I could keep it right there, I would have a respectable time. The course took another right turn and into another climb. Jeepers! The Empire State Building doesn't have this much elevation gain. This feels like an M.C. Escher drawing come to life. Somewhere this course needs to go downhill and when it does I plan on bellywhopping it like Frosty the Snowman.

Finally, the climb ended and was followed directly by a massively steep descent. More appropriately, it was like a cliff dive in Acapulco. Momentum got the best of me and I flailed down the hill desperately trying to keep my feet on the ground. I was giddy to not be climbing, but I felt as if I had taken running lessons from the Ministry of Silly Walks. The road leveled out and my energy was spent. With less than three-quarters of a mile to go, my engine light was blinking. I'd gone from a crisp stride early in the race to a constipated shuffle. The field was starting to pass me at a steady rate. Runners who had paced themselves were effortlessly gliding by me on both sides. My run turned into a walk. I was half a mile away and I was crashing. *Tora! Tora! Tora!* A mother pushing a newborn in a stroller passed me. Seriously? That baby couldn't have been squeezed out more than 24 hours ago and the mother passed me? I mentally switched into the reserves and resumed the running. My stride from the first mile was back and I blazed by stroller mom. A couple of lug nuts fell off a hundred yards later and I was back to the death march. The tortoise comfortably passed me with the child, who I was sure had just stuck its tongue out at me. I mustered one last bit of energy and started to run again. I pumped my arms, desperately trying to generate forward momentum to get across the finish line ahead of my new mocking nemesis. The line was in sight -- only two hundred yards away. I could get there with a four-iron on most days. But my engine had seized for good. I came to a complete stop. I stopped moving. I put my hands on my hips and watched Stroller Mom roll on past me. I resumed my walking towards the finish when a kind-hearted runner slowed down and pointed out that the finish line was just at the end of the entranceway. In my mind, I responded to the Samaritan in a less-than-thankful way.

"Why don't you shut the hell up!"

On Jennifer's checklist of how to make new friends, I am sure that insulting other runners was not very high up.

On March 1, a year and a half after my accident, I reran that same 5k course by myself. The results were less dramatic. I ran around the block thinking how fortunate I was to be able to run at all. I waved and smiled at several neighbors working spring cleanup on their lawns. My body was tired, but in a healthy way. The reduced weight, improved flexibility, and increased training made this run more joyful. Joyful? Running was not very joyful.

Nevertheless, a journey of a thousand miles begins with the first step and I took mine with an eye toward the Barrington triathlon five months away. There were no shortcuts in running. Running is methodical. It is a grind. And, I was beginning to enjoy the solitude of running. My runs started simply and grew to complex routes, as I wanted to explore new terrain.

One more left turn was the mantra I was telling myself as I ran through neighborhoods. One more left turn. One more left turn and I'll have to run another quarter mile to the end of the road. One more left turn and I'll enter the next neighborhood, forcing me to run a half mile back here. One more left turn. Each time I repeated that phrase I could feel an additional surge inside me willing me around the corner. My subconscious was running almost as much as my legs were at that point. My endurance was building. My speed was increasing. My feelings towards running improved to…like.

Chapter Sixteen

More than twenty months into my recovery, I woke to a sobering realization. I couldn't get out of bed. I couldn't raise myself off my own mattress. Even after all the time that had passed, I still had days like that.

The day before, I had done a surf and turf (swim and run) workout. I could feel my back tiring on the way home and by morning I was immobile. It happened less frequently than the previous year, but still no less than every other month.

I pulled my body to the edge of the bed and reached out with my arms to the floor. I tried to imagine slithering like a boa constrictor onto the floor, into the bathroom, and up the wall to the medicine cabinet to get two 800mg tablets of ibuprofen. My chest crashed to the floor. Jennifer heard the noise and knew from seeing my feet still in the bed that I was having back spasms again. The boa gave up. She got out of bed and delivered the medicine to me along with a glass of water. She helped me into my chair, wrapped me in a blanket, and handed me the phone so that I could call out of work. She knew the routine. She invented the routine. Jennifer came back to me a few minutes later before she left for school with the kids and put a warm mug of tea on my table.

"Just relax today."

"Yes, dear."

The ibuprofen, 'horse pills' as we called them, numbed pain as if there was never any pain to begin with and warmed my insides. My mind, previously stressed about missing work and my inability move freely, slowed down. I tilted my head back into the chair and relaxed. The pills made my body feel warm – the way I felt playing volleyball in St. Croix.

I sold timeshare units in St. Croix, USVI for a while in my early twenties. On one of my days off, my boss, Fred McCoy, asked me to pick up two cases of rum, one dark and one light, from the Cruzan Rum factory, located in the middle of the island. The salesmen used the rum as an inducement for the pukes, a horrible term for potential clients, to listen to our spiel about how fabulous coming to St. Croix each year was.

I found my way along the dirt road that led to the Cruzan Rum factory. Most people had seen roads like this in the movies -- roads where the bad guys traveled to execute their victims. The road had a canopy of creepers hanging off the trees that made it seem more like twilight than early afternoon.

The rum factory was decrepit yet colorful, as if a fresh coat of lime green paint could wash away the years of neglect to the structure. The warehouse manager came out to greet me and nodded when I told him I was from Hotel on the Cay. We laughed for a few minutes about the lime green paint and I asked him whether he preferred the dark or light rum. The man told me that there was no difference to him because the company always let him have bottles of both free. However, that day he was partial to the dark because that was what he was drinking with lunch.

"I'll get your two cases of rum. One of each," he said.

"There must be some mistake." I said. "I'm supposed to collect 20 cases of rum, 10 of each."

"No, no, no," the man said, in his rich Caribbean accent. "My paperwork says that it's two cases."

"Sir, why would the hotel have me drive out into the jungle for just two cases? That doesn't make any sense. Heck, I could finish off the two cases before I got back. I'm supposed to pick up ten light and ten dark, or I'm going to be in trouble with the hotel manager. Call Fred McCoy at the hotel. He'll tell you."

The man turned away from me hastily and went back into the warehouse. A few minutes later, he returned and told me to move my van to the delivery dock.

"Yes sir," I said appreciatively.

Ten minutes later, I was heading back down the canopied road with a hundred and nineteen bottles in the back and an open one between my legs.

I always played volleyball on my days off. The sun in January was permanently overhead yet the sand never burned under my feet as I jumped, dove, and spiked on the pitch. I took one of my newly-prized bottles of dark rum and buried it in the sand by the post supporting the net. As we rotated around after each side out, I took a swig off the bottle. The rum grew warm in the sand. With every mouthful I swallowed, I could feel a nuclear pill moving down my throat into my stomach, warming my extremities sending its radiation through my bloodstream. My body was warm. I felt relaxed.

Now, lying in my chair, I appreciated that the horse pills were fast-acting. The knots on my back were soothed with waves of warm oil pouring over my muscles, drowning my pain and dulling my senses. I thought about myself back in St. Croix as a brash young man. I had had no fear of repercussions. If a plan didn't work, I would just move on to the next one. I was more cautious now. Age, children, spouse, job, and a house will make a man more cautious. The young man in St. Croix would be playing volleyball. The man fifteen years older knew that he needed to rest to fight another day.

My back needed time to relax. The spasms were spontaneous, sometimes occurring after a long period of exercise, a twist in the wrong direction or, the worst, from sneezing. I had learned that I needed to assume a hunched-over position, holding onto the edge of a table, to avoid injuring myself during a sneeze. I channel surfed and stopped at a *Law & Order* rerun. Jack McCoy was thundering away at a reluctant witness. I watched with little interest, only biding my time until I could get up without too much pain.

How much longer would I continue to have these godforsaken spasms?

Chapter Seventeen

I needed a bike to race in the Barrington Triathlon, now just three months away. The last time I had ridden a bike was in my early twenties and I was hoping that the axiom about never forgetting how to ride would hold true for me. My trip to a local bike shop in May 2004 put me in front of a salesman who persisted in telling me that I needed a hybrid bike, even after I explained that I was going to do the Ironman.

"How many triathlons do you do a year?" he asked.

"I last raced when I was twenty."

"And you're just going to go out and do an Ironman?"

"Not exactly. I'm going to do a few local sprint triathlons first. Then, I'll do the Ironman."

"I suggest you get the hybrid, in case you change your goals."

I thanked the man for his time and left the store.

My goal was clear, but maybe the path was not. How many triathlons would I need to do before I took on the Ironman? Where would I go to do the Ironman? I normally ignored trivial details, but these details gave me pause. Regardless of where the Ironman took place, I still needed a bike.

Jennifer suggested that I shop online for a bike. This was a period when rumors of internet scams were rampant and ripples of the dot-com bubble burst were still being felt. I went to the only website I could think of which would sell bicycles – Ebay. I found a Tomasso Capri sold direct from the factory for $399. The "some assembly required" disclaimer did not affect my purchasing decision. Buying a bike online was easy, as long as your expectations were low.

My mechanical skills are superior compared to a child building castles with Legos, but for the construction of anything more substantial, they are lacking. Jennifer was concerned about me riding on a bike assembled with my hands. But she was mostly worried about me falling and reinjuring my back. My Spidey senses from ten years of marriage told me that my inability to complete any household project more difficult than screwing in a light bulb was disturbing her.

The bike arrived a week later in a very flat box about the same size as a large painting of flowers that hung on our dining room wall. Sure enough, "some assembly" was required. I recognized the two wheels, parts of handlebars, and a metal tubing triangle, which I assumed was the frame. I began laying out the pieces where I thought they belonged. In fact, the pieces were not where they belonged. Jennifer's voice dripped with sarcasm as she poked fun at my approach.

"Why would *you* need directions? You build these all the time, right?"

As usual, Jennifer was right and I came to my first roadblock when I realized that I didn't own any Allen wrenches. I drove off to the local Ace Hardware to purchase Allen wrenches. I continued to assemble for another hour when I realized that I didn't own any *real* wrenches. Maybe Jennifer was right about my mechanical abilities? Again, I drove to the store to buy tools. My third attempt at assembling the bike seemed to work. At least there were no other types of wrenches to buy.

I took pride in my workmanship and the quality of the ride as I took the bike out for the first time. I pedaled down Washington Road without a helmet, and felt like I was ten years old on Christmas day with my new present. I waved at passersby, feeling proud of my shiny new red bike. I took the turn onto Lincoln Avenue and downshifted to accommodate for the gradual incline. Turning the corner back to home, I sought the lever to put the bike into a higher gear. I searched the entire handlebars, the frame, and the wheels, yet still could not find a way to advance the gears. I would discuss this defect with the mechanical engineer when I got back home, and continued pedaling in the lowest gear. Again, Jennifer was right and the defect was with me. The instructions clearly indicated that in order to shift, you needed to turn the brake clamp inward. I guess I missed the last thirty years in bicycle design.

The first triathlon I had ever attempted was twenty years ago, nearly to the day, in Barrington. It was 1984 and I was seventeen and stupid. I thought that a triathlon was merely an extension of a long swim. I biked to work every day. I ran when I played Frisbee with my friends. Why would I need to do any type of training for the things I did every day? Mostly, I was right. The inherent energy in a growing 17-year-old was powerful enough to carry one through a half-mile swim, twelve-mile bike ride, and three-mile run.

Triathlons were different in the 1980s. First, most of the bikes had bells you rang with your thumb rather than carbon-fiber frames. There were some fancy bikes, but they were all of the road variety. Second, normal people didn't own or wear bicycle helmets. There was a stigma to wearing a bicycle helmet, connoting that one belonged riding the short bus to school. Third, Nike and its 'Just Do It!' footwear campaign hadn't been done yet. Keds and Converse sneakers were everyday shoes, easily transferable to running a few miles at the end of the race. There was no analysis or talk about 'pronating' or 'midstriking.' Frankly, we didn't care. Sneakers went on in the morning and came off just before bed. Fourth, kids back then didn't require a personal water buffalo to keep them hydrated. Most facilities had a bubbler that you could suck a few ounces from, provided you didn't pay attention to the fact they every other kid placed his lips on the same faucet. (In seventh grade, I once imagined I was kissing a girl I liked in school because I used the bubbler right after she did. I tried to get to second base but my teacher pulled my hands off the machine.)

Twenty years later and I was in the exact spot where I had started my triathlon career. No longer was I a spry teenager but rather a man on the mend. I reached across my back, traced my fingers along the scars and looked out into the water not far from where I had been injured. Post-traumatic stress was mostly in the past for me. I now lived with the traumatic stress of stretching my back every morning before I got out of bed. My body had healed considerably in the past two years and I was about to undertake my biggest physical challenge since the accident. Would my back be able to handle the stress of putting all three of these disciplines together? I wasn't sure. The procession of racers moved towards the starting line and my thoughts jumped from whether I was going to finish to how fast I could go. For many competitive athletes, there's a switch that when flipped disconnects fear and turns on rage. In the moments before a race, the mind transforms from paranoid goo to a steel trap, calculating every observable variable. Psychologists most likely would consider this the fight or flight response. Athletes each have their own term. Miles Lane, the noted boxing referee would call it "Let's get it on" time. The Indianapolis 500 announcer would call it "Gentlemen, start your engines" time. AC/DC would call it "For those about to rock" time. Being much less macho than the aforementioned group, I thought of Disney's Darkwing Duck: "Let's get dangerous."

The acids in my stomach erupted, generating a butterfly effect through my chest and then my body. I was going to compete again. The urban legend that says time slows down during important moments of our life isn't true when it relates to starting a sporting event. In fact, it is the exact opposite. The final days before a race move at an increasing speed. The speed of the minutes before countdown increase exponentially. Within a few heartbeats, the start is upon you and the horse springs out of the gate.

A triathlon begins like many other races in that it is a mass start of competitors. However, unlike most races, triathlons offer opportunities for significant injury right from the beginning. Picture the start of a running race, the competitors lined up and a long stretch of road in front of them. Within a minute or two, the tight pack thins out with the elite runners moving to the front and the slower ones lagging. Imagine what would happen if the course took a right turn less than a couple hundred yards away. All of the runners would try to cut off as much of the corner as possible, causing a large bottleneck before the turn. The swim start at a sprint triathlon is much the same, except that while you are at the bottleneck, the person in front of you has the opportunity to kick you in the face. This design causes most athletes (who have an inherent nature to win) to sprint to the turn so they won't be caught in the melee behind the corner. Ultimately, this leads to athletes who are not very good swimmers to sprint to the front and pathetically cause a greater traffic jam.

This scene was eerily familiar to my race twenty years earlier. I remembered being kicked in the jaw back then because I was a faster swimmer stuck behind a slower one. That painful recollection guided me to a different strategy. I would start wide of everyone else and swim around the scrum. However much I wanted to race, I needed to remind myself that I was still hurt and that one event was not worth two days on the couch.

Wisdom, however, is often lost on fools. Following the starting gun, I stayed far to the left in advance of the right turn just one hundred yards into the swim. My pace was stronger than I had expected. I felt as if I was holding the reins on a thoroughbred. I was back in a race and my body was ready to explode with energy. My arms pumped through the water; my breathing and heart rate accelerated beyond a normal comfort range. When I sighted the red turn buoy, I dashed my "stay wide" strategy and maneuvered right into the mix, trying to get to the turn faster than the pack. Unfortunately, my wide start gave the average swimmer additional time needed to beat me to the turn, but I persisted undaunted. I could feel people tickling my toes as they crept up on my position. With each tickle, I employed a crossover kick to ward them off from drafting too close. Just before the buoy, I made my first aggressive move. Similar to a cowboy roping a calf, I grabbed the ankle of the swimmer in front of me and then, with one strong pull, I moved ahead and left him behind me. The key to this trick is not to let the swimmer in front sense that you are approaching. Most swimmers will draft directly behind the swimmer in front occasionally tickling his toes and, in the process, give away his position. I would swim just to the left of the person in front, equal to their lower calf, then reach over, secure the ankle and yank. I often think about the legality of this move, but that comes mostly long after the race. In the heat of the battle, my mind focuses on getting to the clear water ahead of me. I am certain that this is frowned upon in cycling. The Italian racing team putting a stick in the spoke of young Dave in *Breaking Away* does not happen in triathlon racing, but it might be a nice way to help the swimmers.

I finished third out of the water and made my way to the transition area. Most of the racks were full with bikes, leaving me satisfied at my swimming performance, but realizing that I would see them quite shortly passing me on the course. The twelve-mile bike course meandered around the peninsula of Barrington and its many nooks and crannies. With twenty-eight turns, it was a technical course. However, you needed to be at a particular speed for that to matter. Not a problem for my cheap red internet bike and me.

The ride was comfortable and only thirty or so people passed me. Thankfully, the guy whose ankle I grabbed didn't have a big stick as he went by me. The run was a simple out-and-back down the town's wealthiest street. Stunning Victorian houses lined Rumstick Road, casting the perspective that you were smaller against their majesty. At the turnaround, I felt both fear and resolve. Fear because I wasn't sure how much longer my body could keep up the pace. I could feel my legs getting heavy and my breathing labored. Resolve because I raced past being in the dark waters searching for help, past my first steps from the hospital bed, past the electrical stimulation, past breaking scar tissue and past the opaqueness of how I would live my life. The memories of the trauma over the past two years carried me forward until the cheering took over. The finish line was only a football field away. I entered the finishing chute and let a sprinting young man pass me just before the line. I didn't care about my place or my time. I cared that I was alive and that I could finish this race on my legs.

On the heels of completing the Barrington YMCA triathlon and earning a pair of socks for my ninth-place finish in the men's 35-39 age group category, I entered another sprint race two weeks later in nearby Bristol. This race had a very different feel for me. Racing was not rote, but the sense of wonder was gone and my mind was focused on the larger goal from The List, completing the Ironman. Before the start, the sensation of sand slipping through the hourglass still existed. The difference was that I knew before the race that I would finish. The anxiety of wondering if my body handle this test passed and was replaced with a sense of mission.

Following the finish (I did not earn a pair of socks or other clothing), I bellied up to the refueling bar. Most races have the same assortment of goodies -- bagels, bananas, nut bars, and watermelon. Racers gorge themselves with the thought of refueling what they lost during the race, yet completely oblivious that the five-hundred calories they burned during the event pales to the two thousand they are stuffing down within ten minutes of finishing.

I'm a binge eater and if the race organizers are giving away cinnamon raisin bagels then I damn well was going to plow through the entire box. While battling to breathe with my dry mouth, lacking the necessary juices to ingest my fifth bagel, I heard two of the faster racers talking about the half-Ironman they were racing the next weekend. I listened intently as they described the seaside course and the challenges of finishing the thirteen-mile run in the scorching afternoon heat. I wanted to ask a few questions, but my mouth was enraptured with cinnamon deliciousness. They walked away and I convinced myself that I was going to do that race. My body was ready. I was primed. I finished a sprint race with a three-mile run and only had to walk four times to catch my breath.

When I came down from the sugar high an hour later, my senses returned and I realized that it would be foolish to attempt such a feat. A half-Ironman was a rung on the ladder of The List, but it would have to wait…for one full year.

I drove home wanting to celebrate. Jennifer and the kids were not in the house, which was not the worst thing in the world, as it afforded me a chance to shower and take a nap. My body cleansed, my belly still full of cinnamon raison bagels, I put on a rerun of *Law & Order,* but it was scenes of the race that kept replaying in my mind. Two years of work to achieve this triumph. Back when I had been in my hospital bed and unable to walk, it was difficult to see the path I would follow. Now that path was becoming a little clearer each day. I yawned.

I didn't mind being in the house by myself. Some of the best victories in life are celebrated alone. I grew up as an only child and learned to appreciate my own company. I wiggled my toes. This was a successful day. I still had dreams about the propeller. It still hummed in my ear some nights as I tried to fall asleep. I still saw the beer cans and could taste bile in my mouth from my anger. Tomorrow, I would wake up and need to stretch harder and longer just to get out of bed. But today, today was a successful day.

Chapter Eighteen

I began swimming more regularly that winter of 2004, two years after the accident. Old people at the Barrington YMCA liked the water just a few degrees below a lobster boil temperature. The 6 a.m. swim crowd had a cultural dynamic on par with the characters of *The Golden Girls*. At the center was an aged kindergarten teacher named Alice Wood. Alice had a strut resembling an out of shape admiral. She marched from the locker room each morning, jumped into "her" lane and instantly began to swim. Common courtesy in lap swimming would call for the incoming swimmer to wait for any swimmers in the lane to turn at the wall and push off. Admiral Wood didn't believe in such courtesy, that was for Non-Coms.

During my first week, five swimmers occupied the "fast" lane. "Fast" is intentionally in quotations because each would complete one length of the 25-yard pool in just under an hour. Not wanting to play Frogger with these folks, I decided to swim one lane over, with Admiral Wood. Three minutes into my warmup, I stopped at the same wall and caught an earful from the admiral.

"You're not in the right lane. You need to move to that lane," she said, indicating the full "fast" lane.

Most lap swimming is circle swimming, moving up and down the lane in a counterclockwise manner. I offered to the admiral that we split the lane rather than circle swim so we would not have to worry about passing each other.

"Get out of this lane!" she replied.

I smiled, shook my head, and pushed off back down the lane.

The admiral moved to the far lane, exited the pool and marched to the lifeguard. I could see from my breathing side that she was marshalling her troops. The admiral pivoted and returned to "her" lane with the lifeguard in tow. As I approached, the admiral detonated another one of her torpedoes by jumping in the water in front of me and proceeding to swim.

I stopped at the wall where the lifeguard was waiting.

"Will you please move to the fast lane?" he said.

I told him that there were five people in that lane and only one here. He again referred me to the fast lane.

"No."

I faced down the lane and watched the admiral plodding through the water. My ire was up, I was pissed, and I was ready to make some waves.

I swam for the Barrington YMCA swim team for one season in 1983 when I was sixteen, in this same pool. Mark Holmes was a fiery man who coached the team for over ten years. Mark had brought with him the high-blood-pressured intensity of a football coach. He would march down the sides of the pool with purpose, eyeballing each swimmer who breathed in his direction, driving them to push themselves harder. Many swimmers refused to breathe while swimming for fear that Mark would be looking at them. I always thought this strategy was stupid because either you passed out on the bottom or you needed to stop at the wall to catch your breath. Either way, you gave Mark unfettered access to yell at you for not swimming hard enough.

Mark was also an exceptional teacher and would spend time with each swimmer, helping them understand the mechanics of the stroke and how each movement resulted in a more efficient flow through the water. I was in the fast lane with the oldest kids on the team when we received our lesson about using our hips during butterfly. Mark explained that most swimmers didn't drive with their hips during the stroke. Perhaps he failed to appreciate that butterfly is an extremely tiring stroke which might be the reason for hip drive failure. Mark ignored that excuse. He stood on the deck above us and started to slap his hips.

"This is where your power comes from. Right here. You need to visualize that you are fucking a woman."

At that point, I had taken a quick head count of my lane mates and breathed a sigh of relief that they were all male.

"I want you to visualize yourself fucking a woman that's stronger than you. You need to drive those hips hard."

Mark had started to emulate the hip motion required to swim butterfly and not based on real life experience, but from the pornographic movies I'd watched up to that point, the hip motion for sex.

"I want you to picture you're fucking Martina Navratilova. Ugggh! Ugggh! Ugggh!"

Mark started making a series of violent thrusting motions.

"Fuck her hard! Now, let's try that on this next set of 100s. We're leaving on the top."

I had a completely new mindset for how to swim butterfly. I needed to visualize having intercourse with the world's number one female tennis player while on a waterbed. Only now, twenty years later -- on the precipice of swimming butterfly to create a wake to sink the admiral -- did I appreciate the lesbian irony of the drill.

Chapter Nineteen

My motivation to improve on the two sprint triathlon performances in the prior year drove me to train over the winter. The swimming was easy. The pool was inside. The water was warm. Easy. Running became manageable. I was shocked at how easily I shook my craven ways and began to run in the cold. The frigid air would enter my throat and take the elevator down to my chest, the lights flashing as it passed each floor. It was exhilarating.

The winter weather made sleeping difficult. My back was in a constant spastic state as the muscles tightened in the cold. I kneeled on my bed every morning and stretched in the Allah pose before I rose. A couple of times per day I would perform other sets of stretches to keep the muscles loose, but within a short period of time I could feel them recessing deep inside me. ThermaCare back wraps became my couture look. Resembling a men's girdle, the back wrap's charcoal plates activated when exposed to the air, creating a long-lasting source of heat right where Daddy needed it. I became a commercial for the product, even lifting my shirt at dinner parties to show how it fit. That stopped quickly with one look from Jennifer and a stern, "Trent David!"

With the back wrap applied, I would brave the cold for a brisk walk. My back still needed ten minutes of heat and gentle stretching before it would allow me to take any reasonably-sized stride. So, I power walked. Actually, scratch that. Men don't call it power walking. It's walking. Period. I walked. Then I ran.

Running was miles better than trying to bike in the winter. A pair of warmer days passed in February, melting the small amount of accumulated snow and offering a brief window of opportunity to bike in the streets. eizing the opportunity on a windy Saturday afternoon, I bundled my body thoroughly, including my ThermaCare, and proceeded out. The wind was pushing from the north while my path trekked east through Barrington towards the exposed coast. My body was comfortably warm, but my extremities froze within a mile of leaving the house. Even though I dated a meteorologist's daughter in college, she and I never spent time studying wind chill factors, as was now evidenced by my wearing flimsy gloves and open cycling shoes.

The forty-degree starting temperature combined with a twelve-mile-an-hour steady wind and my pushing through the air at seventeen miles per hour resulted in my fingertips turning brittle and on the verge of snapping off like some cheap ceramics. I would occasionally blow on them to get some semblance of feeling back into the tips, but it only lasted for a second before returning to numbness. My ride took me away from town and down windy Mathewson Road, running alongside the narrow Barrington River. My head was down to avoid the oncoming wind when I noticed the pedaling had become more difficult. Looking behind my crankset, I could see that my rear tire had gone completely flat. Drat!

My experience in changing tires was nearly limited to calling AAA. My father made me learn how to change a tire before I could get a driver's license. Now, instead of a crowbar, I carried a pair of modified golf divot tools to help me get the tire off the wheel. Riding with a group of local cyclists on a training ride the summer before, I had met a man, Todd Kenyon, who fixed other people's flat tires. Todd didn't bother with tools to remove the tire; rather, he placed the wheel against his upper thighs and ripped the tire off the wheel. Todd must have had forearms from Zeus. He would rock the tire once or twice then -- *rip* -- off came the tire. He'd replace the tube, place the wheel on his thighs, and reseat the tire, all in less than four minutes. Me, it took four minutes to get off my bike with my ass frozen to the seat. Worse, I couldn't stand. My back was locked into the hunched over position of Quasimodo. I lurched to the back of my bike and struggled to open the pouch containing the tools and tube. My fingers were too numb to hold the tools to remove the wheel; they just fell onto the road in a scattered mess. I tried to summon the will of the Greek God of Tire Changing, but I clearly didn't have the correct sacrifice to offer. Tears froze to the sides of my face as the winds howled up from the river. My choices: running nearly five miles home pushing the bike, riding home and damaging the wheel, knocking on doors and begging for alms, or jumping in the river. I decided to bike home. It was slow and methodical. I hated it. I hated biking. I hated the cold. I hated the pain in my back causing me crooked vision. And, I needed to replace the wheel which bent on the ride home.

I spent the next two days on the couch waiting for the spasms -- caused by biking in the cold -- to release, 800mg of ibuprofen at a time. My upstairs living room overlooked where the accident had happened. It was easy to get lost in the memory of how my body was mutilated, but I tried to fight that sensation. My body was getting stronger, I told myself, even though I was virtually immobile on the couch. I needed to look past the person I was to the person I wanted to be. I needed to recognize that the past could not be so ingrained in me that I was unable to escape its rut. God saved me from the dark water, not to wallow at why I was hurt, but rather to improve the world. First, I needed to improve myself. I was improving -- and I would do more when I could get off the couch.

Chapter Twenty

The sun rises earlier, snowbirds return, tulips bloom, and temperatures turn milder -- these are all signs of spring in New England. A lesser-known harbinger of spring is the first ride of the Wheels of Misfortune (WOM). WOM is a group of middle-aged men whose wit exceeds both their fashion sense and cycling abilities. The group would meet at 5:30 a.m. every weekday morning in front of Ace Hardware in the center of town. Their train passed me early one morning. Ten or twelve of them zoomed by me in a tight, straight line and a blur of vividly colored spandex. And just like that, they were gone.

One of their members approached me at our sons' Saturday morning soccer game, looked furtively around for who was watching and offered me the secret password.

"Show up at 5:30 and ride."

Maybe not so secret after all. I was in the club.

Five-thirty take off time is an early wakeup call when you live a few miles away from the starting line. I woke up at four just to make sure that I had plenty of time. The protocol for team bicycle training was foreign to me. I mastered swimming years ago: jump in, circle swim, and get out of the way if you are on the verge of being passed. There must be some method for riding. How did they stay in a straight line? What speed did they maintain? Did they have Richard Simmons as team fashion coordinator?

The entire elapsed time to dress, prepare, and ride to the start was forty-two minutes, meaning that I left a lot of sleep on the bed. *Next time, Trent. Next time you can sleep a little longer.* The crowd started showing up around 5:20 and introductions were made. Up close, these guys didn't seem like award-winning athletes, or even athletes for that matter, just office guys without the khakis. We left Ace Hardware and rode on the East Bay bike path for a half mile, then turned onto winding New Meadow Road along the beginning of the Barrington River. The bikers moved in a blob with a level of discourse on par with a tepid bridal shower: children this, yard work that, Red Sox the other. Without notice, at least to me, the blob morphed into a spear and the pace, which was already making me breathe a little hard, increased. I fell into line at the back of the pack when the group, I swear, flipped the hyperdrive to light speed. The stars, previously white lights in front of the Millennium Falcon, stretched out in front of me then *POP!* The line of riders was gone.

They pulled away from me at an increasing rate. I watched them move fluidly around a curve where I lost sight of them. As I passed the curve, I could see them in the distance until they rounded another and were gone. One last glimpse of them seemed to be like a distant ship on the horizon then *poof!* I biked for a few more miles on the same road before turning back and heading for home. I would go back again. If I wanted to be able to bike 112 miles in the Ironman, I needed to be able to stay with a pack of middle-aged men. Tomorrow was a rest day. I could only exercise every other day to allow my back time to rest.

Chapter Twenty-One

Sprint triathlons became easier as I learned the nuances of pacing, transitions, and racing strategy. My finishing places improved as well. Reporters weren't asking for interviews yet, but I was in the top twenty percent of the field. In two weeks' time, I would attempt my first Olympic triathlon. The distances would be double those of the sprints: 0.9-mile swim, 24-mile bike and 6.2-mile run.

The Old Colony Olympic triathlon was held in Lakeville, Massachusetts in July 2005. The course consisted of a lake swim followed by four laps of a six-mile loop around the lake and ended with one lap counterclockwise around the lake. For some reason, I was confident that I would do well. Maybe it was the second bowl of Frosted Flakes I had for breakfast or maybe the new aerobars I put on my bike. The clerk at the store told me that I would gain a full mile per hour using them, translating into about four minutes saved on the bike. (With equipment like that who needs to train? Just put a rocket back there.)

I finished first out of the water and made my way to the bike. The transition area required racers to run their bikes down a wooded trail for a short way before mounting. Once on my bike, I grabbed my water bottle and took a long, deep gulp and returned the bottle to its holster…almost. I missed the holster and the bottle bounced behind me and off the road. Oh well, it was only twenty-three more miles until the next rest stop. I could manage.

By the third loop, I actually had passed some people. They must have been far enough behind in the swim that I could catch up on the looped course. I smiled to myself. I passed people on the bike! A car in front of us was turning left. This race apparently didn't yet have the prestige to cordon off the roads entirely. To the car's right were a couple of slower riders attempting to ease by the narrow gap between the car and the curb. I elected to pass the car on the left. There was a volunteer in front directing traffic and, for the moment, holding the car at bay. I yelled to the volunteer to hold the car and made my pass on the left, also passing five or six racers in the process. Back on the course, I settled into my aerobars and kept pumping away. On my left, a motorcycle carrying a passenger passed me. The passenger gave me a hand signal resembling a salute. A congratulations for a well-executed pass. I returned with my best Troop 6 Boy Scout salute and returned to my aero position.

I pedaled for a short while longer, thinking about the motorcycle. Something wasn't right. I couldn't reconcile why the person on the motorcycle signaled me. But for some reason it seemed vaguely familiar. Then I remembered.

In 1984, during the fall of my senior year of high school, the New England area was transfixed with Boston College football. Doug Flutie scrambled and chucked the pigskin towards the Heisman Trophy. On a slow Saturday night at the Cathay Dragon, the restaurant where I worked as a busboy, I watched the Hail Mary pass that Flutie threw to Gerald Phelan against the University of Miami. Flutie spun through the backfield avoiding defenders like a matador. He heaved the ball towards the end zone and the ball's trajectory perfectly guided it over the wall of waiting defenders and into the belly of Phelan. I cheered. That pass solidified my desire to attend Boston College the following year.

Unfortunately for me, one hundred thousand other teenage boys were watching the same game and had the exact same thought. During my campus interview with the Boston College admissions office, the officer told me that applications had increased by a factor of five that year.

"Isn't it amazing what a good football year can do for admissions?" he said.

My A- grade average and 1200 SAT scores lacked the cachet to walk into Boston College. Being an Irish Catholic wasn't going to put the "approved" stamp on my application either. I needed to appeal to the Athletic Department for help. Heck, if football players who read at a third grade level can go to Boston College free, a decent local swimmer that would actually attend religion class should be enrolled.

I met with the Boston College swim coach and we talked for a few minutes about the program and its lackluster history. I told him of my Flutie problem and inquired what help he could give to a young backstroker who was ready to bleed Crimson and Gold.

"None," he replied.

None. The answer was cold and curt. He told me that he already had a solid backstroker and two more were already coming in through early admissions and he didn't need another. My short-lived, overly-hyped dream of becoming a Boston College Eagle was over. My moderate grades and scores proved to be not enough for the "Flutie Bump."

I enrolled at Providence College the next year and quickly began to bleed Black and White, eagerly awaiting the dual meet with Boston College at Chestnut Hill in January. As a Providence College Friar, I was indoctrinated into the vast differences between the orders of priests running Providence College and Boston College. Providence College is run by the Dominicans. The Dominicans, also known as the Order of Preachers, was founded by St. Dominic to preach the gospel and to combat heresy throughout Europe. The order is famed for its intellectual tradition and has been the sponsor of many leading philosophers and theologians. On the other hand, Boston College is run by the Jesuits who are pedophiles. The distinction between good and evil could not be any clearer. At least that's what they taught us at Providence College.

January came and the team traveled to Chestnut Hill. The first race of the dual meet was the 400-yard medley relay, which began with a 100-yard backstroke. Taking my mark in the middle lane, I looked to each side of me to try to identify my enemies. To the left was a boy who looked to be my age. He must be one of those 'wicked smaht' early admission pukes. To my right was their veteran, John Blood. I stared the longest at him.

The race was over in a flash. I beat both Jesuits by more than a body length. The 200 back, later in the meet, was a closer affair. John Blood and I were nearly even at the 175-yard turn, but I had a little more to finish the race and beat him by a full second. At the conclusion of the meet, the two teams stood in line to congratulate each other. When I shook the Boston College coach's hand, I employed the strongest grip I possessed and refused to let him go. I asked the coach if he remembered me.

"No."

"I interviewed with you a year ago and you told me that you didn't need any backstrokers. Well, I just smoked your backstrokers today and I'm not going to lose a race to you for the next four years."

I released my grip and walked away. Nothing else to say and never looking back.

My next chance to beat the Jesuits was at the Big East Championships in February at the decrepit University of Pittsburgh Trees Pool. Coach O'Neill scheduled me to swim three individual events: the 100 back, 200 back and 400 individual medley, plus relays. I swam good races in the backstroke events, setting personal marks in each, and I qualified for the finals in the 100 back, but noticed a quirk in the finals sheets for the 200 back. I was tied for eighth place to the one-hundredth of a second with...John Blood. Well, I didn't lose (as I previously trumpeted to the Jesuit coach), but I also didn't beat him. The curious part of tying for eighth was that only one of us could swim in the finals at night and the other would be relegated to the banana heat (a term of endearment for consolation finals). Being tied for eighth place is different from being tied for twelfth or third or even first. A year earlier, Olympic swimmers Nancy Hogshead and Penny Oleksiak would tie for first in the 100-meter freestyle. The Olympic committee gave both women gold medals. My fate would be different. There would be a swim-off. I had never seen, heard, or conceived of a swim-off before. Essentially, the two swimmers line up, the winner gets to swim with the sharks that night and the loser swims with the minnows. The only difference between this event and a normal race was the packed stands, the two referees per lane, and only two people swimming in a sixteen-lane pool. I felt a sense of drama as I approached the starting block. My moment of vindication had arrived. I would strike a blow against the Jesuits. Representing a tiny college, I felt like David in a Speedo taking on Goliath. Based on the loud cheers from the crowd that greeted Blood's announcement, it was clear that there were more Boston College fans in the audience. The starter directed us into the water. This was my finals. Coach O'Neill said that when it came to swimming finals, you needed to reach into your swimsuit and see what you got. My typical race strategy was to hold back for the last seventy-five and accelerate when my opponent started tiring. My strategy for this race, however, was going to be different from the trials. I was going to take it out fast. Take it out fast and have confidence that pride and adrenaline would finish the race for me.

I set the pace for the first fifty yards, noticing that John Blood was at my hip at the turn. Turning at the hundred, I caught the big scoreboard and read that I was almost two seconds faster than in the prelims and the Jesuit was a full body length down. I could feel the crowd cheering, but I was not sure if it was for the underdog. After hitting the one-fifty, even the refs were cheering. The ref monitoring my lane raised her arms.

Coming off that sixth wall, I learned what it means to reach into your suit. There is a point where you leave your comfort zone and replace it with pain. At the intersection of comfort and pain, you realize that you still have thirty more seconds to endure and that if you push as hard as you have been, the pain is only going to get worse. It was time to reach into my suit. Reach inside myself and decide whether I was willing to suffer or whether I would succumb and capitulate.

I finished strong and beat my preliminary time by three seconds, but more importantly, I beat the Jesuit by more than two body lengths, a humiliating defeat in the world of competitive swimming. The referee standing over my lane was still holding her arm up. Something was wrong! A raised hand was the referee signal for a disqualification. There were only two reasons I knew for DQing in a backstroke race: swimming on your stomach or not touching the wall with your hand. I climbed out of the water and addressed the referee.

"You missed the turn at the one-fifty," she told me.

"Are you sure I didn't graze the wall and it was missed?" I asked.

"You could have driven a boat through that gap," she replied.

I hung my head. I lost. I swam a time that would have seeded me fifth for the finals, but it was for nothing. I DQed and worse, the Jesuit rose from the dead. As I walked to the locker room, John Blood attempted to console me.

Normally, I consider myself a good loser. Maybe I learned to be a good loser from all the years of being an only child and allowing other kids to beat me at sports and games just to have someone to play with. That afternoon I was not a good loser. After John told me that I swam a great race, I punched and broke a mirror in the locker room. I gave myself a good cut on my left pinky that wasn't going to require stitches, but was going to hurt like hell in the chlorine, in the banana heat that night.

Now, in my first Olympic distance triathlon, I was once again about to endure that bitter taste of shock and disappointment. After dismounting my bike and preparing to begin the run, a race official informed me that I was disqualified for crossing the double yellow line. There was no pleading otherwise. That motorcyclist on the course was a race official and the hand signal was apparently anything but a salute. I let it settle in for a moment then asked if I could finish the race. I told them that this was my first Olympic and I wanted to see if I could finish. They agreed that I could continue, but noted that I would not be given a time because of the DQ. Fine with me. I came to finish the event, not for a time or a medal.

The morning July sun put a few logs on the fire and kicked the temperature into the upper 80s. I began to walk shortly after my first mile, potentially a result of low hydration or inadequate training for the pace I held on the bike. I ran intermittently afterwards. Knowing that my time was inconsequential took a significant amount of pressure off me and I got stronger as the run continued. I ran my last mile faster than my first one and finished with a broad smile on my face. Based on the race photos, you would never know that they had kicked me out of the event. Now, standing at the bagel and watermelon line, my mind drifted to kicking this triathlon thing up a notch to the FirmMan half-Ironman in two months.

Chapter Twenty-Two

For a guy who trash-talked an opposing Division I college coach and who had been disqualified twice from events for being a bit too over-competitive, I was feeling remarkably unconcerned about my first attempt at a half Ironman. I would have been lying if I claimed to be nervous because I didn't consider this to be a race. It was a journey. Sure, there were chip timers and electronic bulletin boards showing the results, but the distance of the event made the timing of the race inconsequential. Unlike the 200-yard backstroke, where a missed wall could kick you out of the finals, a slow transition or a tepid-paced mountain climb would only serve to delay the satisfaction of the post-eventbeer. This was a different type of race, where quick and twitchy was replaced by methodical and plodding.

FirmMan was held in Narragansett, Rhode Island. The course contained a 1.2-mile swim, a 56-mile bike, and a 13.1-mile run which meandered through the scenic seaside village in South County. The early September morning air was crisp. A cold front had pushed out a late summer hot spell and replaced it with an early fall nip.

The event started with a long walk...a very long walk. The entrants walked along the shoreline of Narragansett Beach, away from the heavily-trafficked state beach and through the pristine sand of the private Dunes Club Beach. Bizarrely, the walk is almost the full mile-and-a quarter distance of the swim. My toes started turning numb halfway through the walk because of the cold sand on my bare feet. The coldness in my feet sent shivers through my legs and back and I felt energy rushing from my core to relieve the temperature change. The experienced racers wore flip-flops or socks to the start. Note to self: next time I walk this course I'm going to wear some flip-flops -- nice, sturdy, insulated ones.

Racers started to enter the water to warm up their swimming strokes while I sat down and rubbed some warmth into my feet. The race organizer, using a microphone and a squawk box, ordered everyone out of the water. Following several quick announcements, he started a tape recorder and played Whitney Houston's version of "The Star Spangled Banner" through the makeshift public address system. Through the cracked speaker, Whitney sounded like a warbling duck waiting to be shot. Racers in

red, yellow, green, gray, blue, white, and purple caps wad-
dled around in their wet suits listening to the song and
searching for a flag to cast their eyes upon. Collectively,
they looked like a bag of Skittles poured onto the beach.

We organized into our waves and waited for the
gun. The starter pressed a horn which eerily sounded like a
loon call. The first wave of racers hit the water. Wave is an
interesting word in this description because the waves coming onto the shore were breaking at about four feet. I
watched the green caps, the first group, get tossed backwards with each succeeding wave. The crowd around me
grew nervous about the surf. Good. Scared swimmers were
an advantage to me in that they would be assessing how to
proceed into the waves. For me, the strategy is simple.
When you are about to get hit by the wave, dive under to
the bottom and dig your hands into the sand. Then, as the
wave passes, use the bottom to push forward. Four or five
of these and you would be past the break and into calmer
water. Otherwise, you'd progress like that Springsteen
song, "One Step Forward and Two Steps Back."

My wave started and I took large dolphin dives to
get under the waves. It felt more like I was playing at the
beach than at the beginning of a five-hour race. Within a minute, I was past the wave's break and catching racers from
the heat in front of me. There were several hundred swimmers ahead of me after the break. Passing them was like
swimming a slalom course. The swim ended and I had no
idea of my place because of the staggered start. It really
didn't matter; the journey would continue on the bike.

The 56-mile bike ride was relatively uneventful
other than riding into a headwind for the 20-mile return
stretch. Noon was approaching as I started running and the

temperatures were already in the upper 80s. The beachgoers basked in one more September summer day of glory by the shore. The runners shuffled and sweated along the route, past the breeze of the beach. My goal of breaking five hours was in jeopardy following a ghastly finish on the bike into the headwinds coming off Narragansett Beach. My first mile on the run was 7:15, a respectable pace for me, but I could already feel the engine overheating. The final twenty miles of pushing into the wind had sapped a sizeable amount of the reserves and fluids out of my body. The next mile was plus 15 seconds and then the bottom fell out. After the fourth mile marker, I started picking out landmarks to reach without stopping and I was walking more than running by mile six. The heat and humidity were consuming me. I was crashing and I had well more than an hour of running to go. My stomach was churning and I felt as if I was on the precipice of vomiting. *Breathe deeply. Think of a happy place. Think of a place where it's calm and beautiful, where I would feel good, not on the edge of vomiting.*

The happy place my mind found was a memory from my sixth grade field trip in 1979. Our class went to Lincoln Park in North Dartmouth, Massachusetts. Lincoln Park was a second-rate amusement park with a couple of good roller coasters, several spinning rides, and more midway games than I had quarters in my pocket. But, to eleven-year old me, the confines of Lincoln Park held the promise of countless laughs and endless excitement. My class was dominated by girls. Of the twenty-five in the class, only nine were boys. The girls from Bristol's multi-unit School were the exact same cross-section as from many schools across the country, some prettier than others, some more developed than others, and some more outgoing than others.

Sixth grade is a year when wonderful transitions occur in girls, both physically and emotionally. Unfortunately, eleven-year-old boys didn't view a 16:9 ratio as an opportunity, but rather as an annoyance. Often a loud annoyance. However, something must have begun changing inside me because the trip to Lincoln Park ended up very differently than I would have imagined.

The early June morning had all the markings of a beautiful summer day as we loaded onto the yellow school bus and awaited the thirty-minute ride to Lincoln Park. School buses didn't have reserved seats, but by the time you got to sixth grade, you knew exactly where to sit. The coolest guys and the toughest girls got the back few rows. From that vantage point, they could throw paper, food and liquids at anybody in front of them, and feign total ignorance. Ahead of the cool kids were pretty girls and the rest of the boys. As a person always on the fringe of friendship with the boys in my class, I was able to sit in the boys' section, although it was in the front row of the boys' section. Essentially, I was in the girl zone. The bus driver played the local top 40 station on his radio and the scratchy sounds of static and music moved through the middle section of the bus.

Disco was dying. New guttural riffs were being played in the seedy bars of New York, but in small-town suburbia, where Casey Kasem and his "American Top 40" show was a staple after Mass on Sunday, pop music was played everywhere. Nicolette Larson's "Lotta Love" started playing. Even now, all these years later, the song remains instantly recognizable to me by its introductory saxophone note. "Lotta Love" was just like a thousand other catchy pop songs to this eleven year old in 1979. Its status changed when Sheila Fay stood up and started to sing the words.

Sheila was an attractive girl with beautiful black hair, but because her mother was one of the classroom parents, I didn't talk much with her. It's easy to say that it was the mother's fault, but I suppose I didn't talk to many girls in 1979. Sheila stood and started singing, *"so if you are out there waiting, I hope you show up soon. My heart needs relating, not solitude."* I had no idea what those lyrics meant, but watching Sheila standing in front of me, with the sunlight reflecting off the inside of the yellow bus, stirred something inside my chest. I was nervous for no reason other than I was watching Sheila sing. The song lasted forever and Sheila stood in front of me forever. At least until Cheryl Benn stood up and started singing "Tragedy" by the Bee Gees and the moment passed. I found myself looking at Sheila intermittently for the rest of the ride and enjoyed the warm feeling in my chest.

By the time we had arrived at the park, the temperature had reached the mid 80s and the sky had become cloudless. The 6th-grade class of Bristol's multi-unit burst through the gates of Lincoln Park and dispersed throughout the midway. Glen Conway was one of the few friends I had made during that year of school. He was a large kid with a huge warm smile. He would later become one of the state's best wrestlers in the heavyweight division, but for now he was just another chubby kid like me, intent on playing midway games and getting our money's worth on the roller coasters. The five dollars between us didn't last long with the midway sharks booming out their snazzy phrases. "Hey! How about it!" they would call. The money just fell out of my pockets and into their hands. "You get one in and you do it again!" Two-for-one? I loved those games. Stupidly, I didn't hear the first part about getting one in so I never got to do it again. Broke, we walked towards the roller coasters. One of the cool kids in class was faring better at the games than we were. Mark Woodard showed us a mirror he'd won which had a print of the band Bad Company on it and a green leaf. Mark told us that the mirror would be good for doing lines.

"Super," I said, not knowing that he was an actor.

Mark told me once that he had been doing speed since the third grade. Possessing nothing but a fat ass, I wished I had some speed so I could keep up when we played tag at recess.

Glen and I hustled through every line and turnstile to get on and off the Comet as quickly as possible, to get in as many rides before the lunchtime headcount. The Comet was a typical wooden roller coaster, the type that rattled your teeth from the car jarring on the rails. The Comet was massive and intimidating to sixth-graders mainly because the lap bar never dropped fully into your lap, leaving the skinny kids with the feeling, real or imagined, that they would fall out of the car at every turn. Because of my chub, I normally didn't have this problem, but when riding with Glen, the bar stopped at his stomach line and not mine. For the first time in my life I got the thrill of "nearly" falling out of the car on every ride.

After Glen and I had our fill of the Comet, we sat down on the grass and had lunch with our classmates. This was one of the best days a sixth-grader could have. Playing midway games, riding roller coasters, feeling a throbbing in my chest from Sheila's song, and now eating the most delicious peanut butter and jelly sandwich in the world. How could life get any better, I thought, as I lay on the grass and listened to the sounds of kids screaming on Monster Ride.

After completing our requisite lunchtime break, Glen and I set out to ride The Whirl, one of those rides with two people per cart that spins around with slight up-and-down movements.

It didn't take more than thirty seconds into the ride before my stomach started to feel queasy. The ride was spinning and I decided that by just breathing deeply I would be able force the sensation to pass until the end of the ride. That decision came at the same time Glen said to me, "Now comes the best part of the ride. We go backwards." My face went white with terror. The emotions of the day raced passed by me. The Comet, the peanut butter and jelly, the mid-80s heat, the carnival games, the peanut butter and jelly, and the damn anxiety I felt from watching Sheila sing *"my heart needs protection and so do I."* My body exploded and the undigested, formerly delicious peanut butter and jelly sandwich came up and out and into the hair of the girl in the cart in front of me. She was an older girl with kinky hair which now had peanut butter and jelly mixed in. With the reflexes of a panther, she twisted around to paw at me but couldn't reach. Whew! The safety bar saved another life. She screamed at the top of her lungs, words that I never knew existed and some which I still don't know what they mean. But, I clearly understood the one sentence she kept repeating as the ride slowed down.

"I'm gonna kill you, motherfucker!"

I got the gist of that sentence pretty well.

"I'm gonna kill you! I'm gonna kill you!"

The piercing sounds of her screams rang in my ears. Such a departure from Sheila's beautiful voice. The second the ride ended, Glen and I forced the bar open and we ran down the midway away from the violent screams of the girl with the PB&J hair gel. For the first time in my life, I ran fast, faster than I ever imagined I could run. I guessed that was what Mark Woodard felt like when he took speed.

The change in terrain snapped me back to the present. My pace had improved over the last two miles as my mind was focused on 1979. The final quarter-mile of the race was run on the beach surface. My strides turned into slides as my feet lost footing in the soft brown sand. I was nearing the end of my first half-Ironman. Somehow, I had avoided vomiting and I was running along the beach to the finish line.

The crowd was large as I came within 100 yards of the finish. Haley and Max were standing in the middle of the path waiting for me to arrive. I grabbed each one by the hand and they pulled me through the finishing chute. My children were cheering for me as we ran. They were proud of me. I had made my children proud of me. I felt profound satisfaction at being able to share that moment with them.

A rush of relief passed through me as I crashed into the wall just past the announcer's tent. A volunteer bent down and took off my racing chip and I ambled back towards the finish line to my awaiting family.

A couple of hours later, I was lying on the beach. My stomach was full of pasta, burgers, beer, and the satisfaction of completing the toughest challenge of my life. My brother-in-law, who came to watch the finish, leaned over to me and asked if I was ready to sign up for Ironman Florida, a race that would be twice the distance I had just completed. It was nearly three years to the day since my accident. Three years of pain, tears, suffering, and the insurmountable joy of being alive.

"Hell, yes, I'm doing the Ironman next year!"

Chapter Twenty-Three

Did you know that men bleed from their nipples? I didn't -- not until I reached mile 15 of my longest training run a month before my marathon. My chest started hurting during my planned 18-mile training run. Looking down, I noticed that on the left side of my chest, my jersey was soaked in blood. We lived in a safe neighborhood. When did I get shot? The red stain emanated from the nipple region of my shirt. I lifted the shirt and still couldn't make out where the blood was coming from, at least not until I touched my nipple. That's when it became obvious.

Bloody nipples weren't the only bit of nastiness that greeted my introduction to endurance running. Over the months, I found that certain leaves were more comfortable than others when diarrhea strikes in the middle of a trail run. I learned that most homeowners would give you a drink of water if you asked. I experienced that new sneakers were great to wear but not for the first time on a twelve-miler. Now, I could admit that I'm a nipple bleeder.

I thought the pain of bleeding, not to mention the embarrassment of running through my neighborhood with a pair of oddly-located bloodstains on my shirt was bad enough, but it paled in comparison to showering. When the water hit my nipples, it felt like I was in the Georgia State Penitentiary where they were firing up Old Sparky to mete out my punishment. The water struck me as if it carried 2,000 volts at 7 to 12 amps.

My back still wasn't good with the running. The pounding stride after stride was taking a prolonged toll on me. Each morning after a run, I needed to roll over in bed onto my knees and stretch for ten minutes to get me loose enough to walk down the stairs. Autumn and its colder temperatures also aggravated my back. I began to wear thicker protection around my lower back to keep it warm. The colder temperatures made me lean more each day. Jennifer could see the grimaces on my face as I would try to straighten up each day. She wanted to tell me that the pain I was inflicting on myself was hurting her to watch. The juice was not worth the squeeze. She kept those comments to herself out of respect for me. She knew how I revered this journey and the goals I had set for myself. What I didn't appreciate in the moment was how selfish The List was. The List didn't massage my back when I was hunched over. The

List didn't carry me up the stairs when I ran out of strength. Jennifer did these things. She knew I was being selfish and she accepted my selfishness because of her love for me.

With Jennifer muting her concerns, I set out to cross off The List's eighth item -- completing all 26.2 miles of a marathon. I set my sights on the 2005 Bay State Marathon for the sole reason that it was advertised as "The Flattest Marathon in The East." Running a marathon was enough torture that I did not need to compound it by running up and down mountains. This was only the second non-sprint road race of my life, the first being a ten-miler earlier in July. My goals were simple; finish and, if possible break four hours. There was no reasonable expectation that I would finish within four hours, but I needed some target to keep me focused and that was good enough. The pace of my training runs were all between eight and eight-and-a-half minutes per mile. A four-hour marathon was a nine minute per mile pace, meaning that I padded a little cushion for incidentals.

I trained each weekend with a friend from town, David Werbel. I had met David during a morning bike ride and took an instant liking to him. He was a few years younger than me and had a boyish charm which made him seem even younger. David and I were very compatible in both demeanor and training pace. We discussed essentials about endurance racing on the practice trail and both agreed on one fundamental principle before running a marathon: the second shit was mandatory. In other words, the morning's first movement is vital, but equally important is the thorough cleansing that comes from the second movement. It helps avoid abdominal cramping later in the day. Ah, the stupid things guys talk about when left alone.

On race day, I checked in, secured my bib number to my chest, attached the timing chip and made my way to the Porta Potty. Race directors never seem to get the correct ratio of johns to athletes, as evidenced by skinny people standing ten deep in thirty-degree temperatures waiting for their turn. In the back of my mind, I heard grains of sand passing through the hourglass, but I was fully committed to, and visualizing (as all of the best high-performing athletes do), following through with the morning's second shit. I listened to the swelling crowd laughing and joking with each other. There is a friendly tone at the beginning of running races that is not present in triathlons. Perhaps it's that runners are generally nice people and triathletes are prima donnas. Or…the stall opened and thoughts of pleasant runners dashed from my mind as I got busy with the task at hand. David was right. That may well have been the most satisfying shit of my life. The moment of relaxation coupled with the vacating of all my toxins put me in a serene and satisfied mood.

Just as I was finishing, I heard the announcer's voice blaring over the loudspeaker.

"One minute to the start!"

"Shit!" Bad word choice.

Now I was under some serious pressure. I cleaned up and hopped out of the stall. Where were all the people? There was virtually no one left in line. Memo to self – don't act as if you're reading the Sunday Boston Globe in the toilet next pre-race.

When I finally made it to the starting line, I wound up in the back of a crowd of about 5,000 runners, right back there with people using walkers and crutches. I imposed my size on the skinny runners and pushed my way forward, closer to the four-hour pace group. The gun went off and I felt a push from the back with no movement at the front. It was like sitting at a traffic light that's turned green yet the cars haven't moved. Rationally, you could see that there were ten cars ahead of you that needed to move first, but that didn't stop you from cursing at the traffic for not moving. Let's go, people! Time's wasting!

The first few miles of a marathon are aggravating because you are constantly darting around people who did not seed themselves properly. Either they can't hold a four-hour pace or they are ignorant as to where they should start. Regardless, I felt like I was riding a pogo stick as I bounced from side to side. I couldn't believe that I was actually running a marathon. I guess I always had such a low perception of myself as a runner that I never visualized myself in this position. Meeting people who had finished a marathon was awe-inspiring to me because I couldn't fathom the magnitude of the effort. And now I was in the middle of 5,000 people sharing this journey. I was impressed that all those people worked hard to gain entry to get to the starting line.

I admired Oprah Winfrey for running the New York City Marathon mainly because of her weight. The challenge of carrying that amount of extra weight for nearly five hours must have been exhausting, but she prepared her body to finish. That made me create one of the race strategies I was employing at Bay State called "Follow the Chick with the Fat Ass" strategy. My theory is that if she could do it, so could I.

I settled into my pace at mile two, positioned right behind a young woman with a rotund rump. There was no headwind to speak of and the pace felt faster than training. The Bay State Marathon hosts both a marathon and a half-marathon which start at the exact same time and along the same course until mile four where the shorter race turns off. That's where I stopped following the bouncing butt. She turned, leaving me relegated to following narrow skinny asses, each of which seemed to be moving faster than I was.

I started to include walking into my routine at mile ten. My back was tight, making longer strides challenging. Several times I stretched my hamstrings to relieve some of the pressure, which worked for a mile or so until the spasms returned. At mile twenty, "The Wall" was printed on the road which I thought was an incorrect use of the Pink Floyd catalogue. "Comfortably Numb" would have been a better choice to represent my mental state. What sadists sign up for these things? The self-pity didn't last long because my mind circled around to why I was running and what was coming. I was running because three years ago I couldn't walk. My heart filled with pride every time I visualized my toes at the end of the bed, completely unresponsive while being stroked by the morning nurse. That's why I was running. Because I could. I will finish this marathon. And I will finish this marathon in less than four hours.

The final stretch was down Pawtucket Boulevard, a long straight road alongside the mighty Merrimack River. My body was breaking down. I was undertrained, having gone five miles past my longest run ever. The crisp fall breeze was blowing at my back, like in the old Irish saying, except I didn't think the poem included leaves blowing faster than I was running. Recently fallen leaves danced down the road seemingly unencumbered by gravity. I tried to focus on a leaf and run alongside it, but I couldn't keep up. The leaf was winning the foot race. Two turns before the finish I spotted a man in a wheelchair encouraging the runners. My heart leapt into my throat. I was barely moving forward down the road and I could isolate his voice. It was deep and guttural. He was enthusiastic, bundled in a thick sweater with a scarf. I stopped when I reached the man, which isn't saying much because I was barely shuffling at that point, and thanked him for his support. He looked very uncertain as to why I was stopping and sharply told me that the finish line was just around the corner. I smiled. Yes, it was. Thank you. A surge of energy coursed through me and I ran. I ran like it was the beginning of the race. I passed the zombies that passed me over the last mile, made the turn, and headed into the Lowell Spinners baseball stadium.

Unbeknownst to me, the finish line was NOT just around the corner. The runners needed to enter the stadium and run a lap along the outfield's warning track and then cross home plate. It was a cruel torture because I could see every runner with their head turned towards home plate, fixated on the finish line. The stadium's sound system was blaring Kanye West's "Stronger," an appropriate song. "Now that don't kill me can only make me stronger, I need you to hurry up now 'cause I can't wait much longer." The energy of the stadium made me float towards the finish. Kanye was pumping in my eardrums. I was singing as loud as my lungs would allow. I looked at the clock as I crossed the line. I finished, in 3:58.29, a minute and a half ahead of my goal, but, more importantly, I crossed number eight off The List.

The volunteers wrapped me in a tin foil blanket that made me and the other runners look like baked potatoes. One girl asked for my running chip. I humbly replied that I couldn't bend down and asked if she would remove it for me. More marathoners finished behind me. No longer zombies, each had a look of satisfaction on their face. Jennifer and the kids were screaming at me from the front row of the stands. My pain washed away and I felt myself start to cry. I'm not sure if the tears were because my family was there. Maybe it was because I was there for them. Regardless, it's difficult for a man to cry in front of his children and I moved towards the dugout exit.

Chapter Twenty-Four

The family woke up early on the Sunday morning exactly 365 days before the 2006 Florida Ironman. It was registration day. My dialup modem most likely lacked the sophistication to hack into any government agencies. I was only hoping that I could hold the connection long enough to register and have my credit card charged.

It took several attempts on the website for a spot to open. When the spot opened, I typed like the valedictorian of the Evelyn Wood School and filled in the questionnaire with lightning speed. My mouse hovered over the "confirm" button. I looked at Jennifer and asked,

"Are you sure?"

"Are you sure?" she responded.

"Are you sure?" I repeated.

We had played this game before many years ago. She had the same look of excitement on her face as she had over ten years ago when we were deciding to get married.

At 25, I was directionless. My career could barely be called a career, maybe not even a job. I rented apartments to low-income families when there wasn't something better to do during the day like...take a nap.

We were sitting in the parking lot of Malabar Grove, Jennifer's place of employment in East Providence. I had picked her up after work to go out for dinner and we had returned to get her car. The question wasn't resolved during dinner. It was me. I lacked the courage to ask her to marry me. I was scared of the changes in my life which were about to begin and I was too immature to think the events through rationally. Jennifer looked me squarely in the eye, paused a second or two for effect and to make certain that she had my complete attention.

"Why don't we propose to each other?" she asked.

That was a novel idea. In what seemed like nanoseconds, my synapses connected that this approach would save me from planning an elaborate proposal ceremony with rose petals spread across a finely-combed beach at sunset. Or, some other half-baked hopelessly romantic scheme I might come across.

Jennifer stared intently in my eyes. There was a look of determination mixed with frustration, most likely from my current display of cowardice. Jennifer asked if I was ready, then took a shallow breath through pursed lips.

"Repeat after me. Will."

"Will."

"You."

"You."

"Marry."

"Marry."

"Me."

"I'll have to think about it."

There was a nervous pause in the air, like stepping off a cliff without actually falling. I didn't see her fist coming in the darkness of the car. It wasn't until my head completed its 720-degree spin on my neck that I realized she had hit me. The next few words out of her mouth may not be considered proper for a normal engagement ceremony, or even a Hell's Angels convention. My cheek was swelling and I backed my body position as close to the door as the fastened seat belt would allow. Adrenaline pumped through my body and was sending the fight or flight signals to all listening organs.

"Me. Me. Me. Me. Will you marry me? Will you marry me?"

My words sputtered out between her visceral epitaphs denouncing me as scum or shit or something like that.

"Will you marry me?" I repeated.

Her face changed. She underwent a metamorphosis back from Mr. Hyde back to Dr. Jekyll and she batted her eyes. Her voice relaxed and in her typically songbird way she said yes and hugged me.

Now we were at the computer as I hesitated committing to Ironman Florida.

"Are you sure, Jennifer?"

"Absolutely, you've come a long way for this moment."

And with that, I pressed 'confirm,' and shouted out loud.

"We are going to the Ironman in one year!"

Without prompting, Haley began to sing "Seasons of Love," from the musical Rent.

"Five hundred twenty-five thousand six hundred minutes."

Jennifer and I promptly joined in.

"Five hundred twenty-five thousand moments so dear."

Max had never heard the song before, but that didn't stop him from dancing around the dining room where we were sitting.

"In daylights, in sunsets, in midnights, in cups of coffee, in inches, in miles, in laughter, in strife."

We sang and we laughed. We danced and we rejoiced. Our family was together, healthy and in love.

Later in the afternoon, I sat by myself in the living room under a blanket, imagining the future. Jennifer came in after a while and joined me under the covers. I remembered something which I needed to remind Jennifer. I did not divulge a small secret to you, the reader, earlier. When the family returned to the house following the half-Ironman, the kids went to the family room to watch a movie while Jennifer and I went upstairs to make love. I thought it was heroic of me to perform after a grueling day. Jennifer was less than satisfied. Regardless, I bragged to her that I was now a quad-athlete, perhaps the only one. Further, I said that she better be prepared for the finish of the Ironman because they may want to put me in the record books.

I reminded Jennifer of this ambition while we were under the covers. She was nonplussed.

"They write about that stuff all the time in Cosmo. You'll need to do better."

Better?

"Trent, you have enough to worry about just getting through the race. Why don't you focus on that?"

Then she left me alone under the blanket.

I did have a lot to focus on. What had I gotten myself into? Five hundred twenty-five thousand six hundred minutes can pass awfully quick.

Chapter Twenty-Five

Eleven months passed with lightning speed. During the year, I finished three triathlons - a sprint, an Olympic, and a half-Iron. Max lost his front teeth, we welcomed two puppies into our family, Haley was on the verge of becoming a teenager, and Jennifer repeated the fifth grade (which is common for a fifth-grade teacher). I trained for my Ironman, averaging just 7.4 hours per week. The books and blogs I had read about training said that the typical athlete will average 15 hours per week with peak weeks of 25 hours. My back kept getting stronger, but I still could not run or bike two days in a row without spasming for a day.

My brother-in-law Michael Hines was also going to Florida to race and he provided me with his checklist. It outlined in detail each part of the race, the pre-race and post-race. I realized quickly that there was more to the race than just competing; it required detailed planning and a system for accomplishing my goal. The race was over 1,300 miles away and I needed to organize how I was going to get and return from the event with all my gear, in addition to the longer transitions of the Ironman. I sat down with the checklist and tried to think of the best way to prepare.

Preparation, when I was younger, was not my forte. Even before I took my first paid job, I already had a work nickname. My parents disrespectfully, yet accurately, labeled me as "half-job." My father bestowed the moniker on me for my uncanny ability to start any project and find myriad reasons to stop: I had to check the Red Sox score, I thought I heard my friends calling, I wasn't feeling well, I had to go study (especially useful during the summer).

My reputation notwithstanding, I was hired as a dishwasher at the Lobster Pot, a seafood restaurant on the shore of Bristol Harbor. Eugene McCarthy greeted me at the entrance of the restaurant. I was an hour early for my shift and he looked incredulous at my arriving so early. Most high-school dishwashers were a coin toss as to whether they would show up at all.

"I thought you were selling subscriptions or something," he said, taking delight in teasing me.

He smiled and his ocean blue eyes gleamed in the glow of the poor kitchen lighting.

"Well, seeing as you're here, I might as well show you around."

The entire kitchen and restaurant were still empty. I guessed the rest of the crew didn't believe in the 'hour early for work' rule I had made. Mr. McCarthy showed me my post and went through the mechanics of working the dishwasher.

"Now, any moron can open and shut the dishwasher, but effective dishwashers create a process for taking in the dishes, moving them through the machine, stacking them and replacing them."

He opened the machine and inserted an empty rack into the steamy box, then closed the box and pressed the large red button on the side of the machine.

"Before you wash a single dish I want you to think of a process to do your job effectively. If you get behind, it has a negative impact on the rest of the kitchen. I won't have enough dishes. Customers won't have lobsters to eat, you won't have dishes to wash, and I won't need you."

He opened the steaming machine, pushed the empty rack down the line, and replaced the void with another rack, pressing the red button after he closed the machine.

"So, I want you to stand here and figure out the process which will be most effective."

I nodded. I understood my mission. I looked around at my surroundings, ran my hand along the clean smooth stainless steel dish collection area, noting that it would stay forever clean. And it did -- for the next two hours. I stood for the next two hours defending my post without a dish to be washed. Finally, Lucy, a rotund, seasoned waitress, brought me my first two dishes. Two salad bowls. I promptly attacked the two dishes. The opening salvo in my climb up the corporate ladder. I scrubbed the dishes, re-scrubbed them, slid them into the washing box, pressed the red button and waited. Forty-five seconds later the dishes were done. I opened the box, dried the dishes and brought them to the dish rack. It was then that I noticed how many different types of dishes there were. I asked Beth, the comely prep cook with dyed blonde hair, to explain to me what all the different types of dishes were for.

"Well, these three are for salads, these two are for appetizers, these are for littlenecks, these are for lobsters, these are for fish, these are for fries, these are for butter, these are for bread, these are for coleslaw, these are for non-fish entrees, and these are for desserts."

I think Beth described that entire roster of dishes in only one breath. Just looking at the variety of dishes took my breath away. Another waitress, I didn't get her name, dropped off four salad bowls into my fortress. Lucy snuck in some appetizer plates and silverware right behind her.

I returned to my post and proceeded to attack the invaders. After I had completed each batch of dishes, I took a long sip off my Coke. That was one of the fringe benefits of working in this illustrious establishment -- free Coke. By 7:30 p.m., the restaurant was jammed. There was a crowd at the bar waiting to be seated, the dishes were piling up, and my hands were moving like Neo in the Matrix thanks to the seven Cokes I'd slammed in the past two hours. The caffeine started coursing through my body and I began vibrating at my post.

I continued scrubbing dishes and packing them into the machine, but the dishes were clashing and didn't fit. It was like I needed a Ph.D in Tetris to figure out how to stack those dishes. The more I struggled the more the dishes piled up.

"You're getting in the weeds, boy," Lucy informed me.

Weeds? I felt like I was getting caught in the Amazon. The harder I pushed to get dishes through the machine, the slower I was moving. Beth came over with a dish and handed it to me.

"I can't serve dinners on dishes that have fish guts caked on."

She was smiling at me but it was a worried smile.

I broke a couple of glasses and needed to stop the dishes to get the pieces out of the sink. On second thought, maybe the shards would slice my veins and I could die slowly at my post.

"We're out of lobster dishes," Edna screamed.

Edna had the lovely disposition of a malaria-carrying mosquito. She would annoy you, annoy you, annoy you, and finally bite. And, there wasn't any type of spray you could use on her. Edna was responsible for expediting the orders, or more simply, she was in charge of putting food on the dishes before they were taken to the customers. Edna didn't waste a second in informing Mr. McCarthy that the production line was going to stop because of me. I looked around and asked about the extra lobster dishes on the shelf.

"Those are for emergencies," Edna said.

Dammit woman, can't you see we've got an emergency here? I was being overtaken by the ceramic Huns. I needed reinforcements. Were those extra lobster dishes on some sort of National Guard Reserve program? If so, we needed to call them up to active duty.

I must have said this out loud in my frustration because Mr. McCarthy promptly came from behind his stoves and walked over to my collapsing fortress.

"Edna tells me that we're out of lobster dishes," he said, calmly and quietly.

I pointed to the stack on the wall and told him that we could use those while I caught up.

"Those dishes are for an emergency and this is not an emergency. We are out of lobster dishes because you did not figure out a process to do your job. That and I think you're high on Coca-Cola."

I nodded involuntarily twelve or thirteen times.

"Why don't you go back and run me some lobster dishes?"

I continued to nod and returned to my post. I scrubbed twelve lobster dishes, put them into the machine.

"Now, appetizer plates."

I started scrubbing appetizer plates. Finally, it occurred to me what I was doing wrong and how best to fix it. Scrubbing the salad dishes, I discovered the Rosetta Stone for dishwashers: don't wash dishes as they come in, wash dishes in sets. After that, the job was easy.

Mr. McCarthy came to visit me after the kitchen closed. The kitchen typically closed an hour before the dishwasher was done and he outlined for me the work that needed to be completed before I went home.

"Did you find out the process that is most effective?" he asked.

"Yes," I told him.

"Good," he replied. "You should consider doing that same type of evaluation on the first day of every new job you start."

I thanked him for the advice and continued with my shift.

Mr. McCarthy was correct about learning a process. I've applied his lesson to every job I ever started. Most people try to rush into completing a task or two, but I've found that, if you just sit there and think about the overall objective, you'll achieve it much quicker.

I saw Mr. McCarthy right after my first marathon, twenty years later, at a golf course in St. Augustine, Florida. He was working as the course's starter. His face was weathered and he looked significantly older, but his ocean blue eyes were as vibrant as they were in my youth. I reintroduced myself and told him how I had profited from his simple lesson throughout my career. He smiled, then burst out with a raucous laugh. He remembered me vividly.

"You're the boy who wanted to call in the National Guard of plates. I've told that story a hundred times."

It's funny. You think that someone has made an indelible, lifelong impression on you only to find out that you've done the same to them.

Now, with a race that was going to take place a thousand miles away and cover 140.6 miles, I needed to sit back at that dishwashing station and plan for the challenge. I continued to review the checklist and realized the best way to prepare for this race. I made a few notes about how I would pack, how I would lay out my gear, and how I would transition between events.

Michael and I brought our bikes to Newton, Massachusetts to have them transported to the race via an eighteen-wheeler. What a novel idea! The rig trucked down the east coast, picking up bikes along the way, delivering them to the race, and would do the reverse on the return. Transporting the bikes removed a huge obstacle from the planning process.

Chapter Twenty-Six

started race day with two bowls of Honey Bunches of Oats. My wife is great. Who else would run to Walmart to buy me my favorite cereal? It was November 2006, just over four years since the accident and I was an hour away from attacking number nine on The List. I ate my breakfast on the veranda and watched the choppy waves in the Gulf of Mexico. The air was cold, maybe somewhere in the 40s. Unfortunately, cold racing gear was not on the checklist. I thought this was the Sunshine State, where snowbirds came to die. Today, the snowbirds would freeze in their birdbaths.

Jennifer woke up shortly after me with a look that demanded coffee. She joined me on the veranda and shivered alongside of me.

"The water looks choppy," she said.

"Yup, a lot of people are going to be intimidated by the swim. That's good for me."

I was kind of hoping that some of the faster ones would be scared enough not to swim, but I knew better.

I finished breakfast and collected my bags. There were five bags in all. As part of the Ironman Mensa Test, you needed to properly coordinate your colored bags so they could be dropped off at the correct location. Nowhere in my nine months of training did I ever practice labeling and organizing color-coordinated bags. Invariably, I kept checking each bag to make sure that I hadn't added or left something vital out of each one, like my brain.

We made our way down to the transition area to drop my bags off and watched the busy bees making final adjustments on their bikes. Racers pumped up their tires, taped nutrition packets to their frames, topped off their fluids. I laughed because I couldn't understand how much Gatorade solution could have evaporated since they topped off the previous night. Some racers were just compulsive. I think that is a defining quality of every racer. We're all compulsive about something. Why else would we be willing to sit on the same seat for five to eight hours straight just to look forward to a marathon? I watched one younger man scrubbing his chain set with a toothbrush. Evidently, there was one little speck of grease which was going to cause a drop in average speed from 21.2 miles per hour to 21.19999. I offered him some Crest, but he had his game face on and blocked me out.

I dropped off my special needs bag at the check-in table. The night before, I had made a couple of jokes about my colored bag fashion show, but as the hour drew near, I started having serious reservations about what I had included in each bag. Racers are given two special needs bags: the first will be dropped off at around the 75-mile mark of the bike course and the second will be dropped off at around the halfway mark of the marathon. Racers put all types of essentials into the race bags including GUs, crackers, drinks, solutions, pills, candy, nuts, sandwiches, and assorted snacks. One racer told me she put tampons in her special needs bags. Dear God, what was this race going to do to me?

I filled my special needs bag with plain vanilla extras -- peanut butter crackers and GU. The seriousness with which the other athletes dropped off their bags, weighing anywhere from 12 to 18 pounds, made me feel like I should have added a couple of dumbbells in case I needed to squeeze out a few shoulder presses to keep loose on the bike.

The next table was the drop-off for the transition bags. These were the bags that contained the most vital racing attire. The swim-to-bike and the bike-to-run bags held every stitch of race clothing and paraphernalia you owned. I was about to hand my bag to the volunteer when a diminutive female racer cut me in line. She bounced on the balls of her feet as she handed a gallon jug of Jergen's lotion to the volunteer, asking him to put the lotion in her bag. The volunteer explained that the bag had already moved to a holding area. The racer pleaded that she needed the lotion to ease her abnormal chafing. The two bantered about where to put the lotion. Put the goddamn lotion in the bag!

I screamed in my head. Silence of the Lambs humor wouldn't go over well. Too many Clarice Starlings and not enough Hannibal Lecters. There were many things I needed to concern myself with and the disposition of her abnormal chafing wasn't one of them. I dumped my bags on the table and walked away.

Twenty minutes until the start of the race. Where had the last hour gone? There are hours in your life that last for days, like the ones I spent in the hospital, unable to move my legs. And, there are hours that pass like a whisper, quiet and almost non-existent. I took off my morning clothes, put them into the final bag, tied the top, handed it off to the nearest volunteer and began the walk around the hotel towards the beach. I was out of bags and I felt a little naked. The only possessions I would have for the next hour were my wetsuit, goggles, cap, and my skimpy 1980s-style racing suit. Let's get dangerous!

Jennifer helped me snake into my three-quarters sleeveless wetsuit. She zipped me up, gave me a kiss on the lips, and told me she was proud of me. Knowing that she supported me gave me the warmest feeling in my heart. Jennifer had been my rock since the accident, nursing me back to health and now standing with me on the verge of crossing this mammoth item off The List.

The competitors filtered onto the beach from all directions. Waddling like Emperor penguins towards the starting line. Dozens of swimmers warmed up in the choppy waters and hundreds sought help to get zipped up. An announcer said the race would start in five minutes and a surge from the back of the pack pushed everyone towards the shoreline. The atmosphere was palpable with nervous kinetic energy. The pros started first and I watched them sprint into the surf. Some pros chose the high hurdle method of getting deeper into the gulf while others dragged their legs through the oncoming waves.

More amateurs entered the water to warm up as I moved my way to the front of the pack. I pushed and squeezed between dozens of rubberized racers on my way to the shore. One racer asked me if this was my first Ironman.

"Yes, it is."

"Enjoy this moment," he said. "Following the start, you may wish that you never signed up."

Undaunted, I made my way to the second row. I wasn't so ostentatious that I commanded a front-row starting point. The man to my right asked me how I was going to do in the swim. I told him that I expected to win the swim.

"Do you know what they call the winner of the swim at the Ironman?" he asked.

I shook my head.

"A loser. Nobody cares about the swim."

And with that comment, the excitement left me for the better part of a minute.

The announcer revved me up when he told us that we were only one minute from the start. The crowd pushed forward and someone three rows back fell over, toppling several other racers in the process. Thirty seconds. How was this crowd going to react? Were they going to ease into the water, knowing they had a 10+ hour day ahead of them, or would they try to take control of the race immediately? Twenty seconds. Most racers hunched over and placed their specially-trained forefinger on the start button of their watches. I couldn't understand this. Why in a 140.6-mile race did you need to start your watch with such precision?

"Let's count down from ten – nine – eight – seven – six – five – four – three – two – one."

BOOM!!!!!

The cannon roared and 2,500 people surged from the rear to get into the water.

It was a sprint to get out into the open water. Hundreds of arms and legs flailed around me. The water bubbled like we were boiling lobsters. I was swimming on top of people, pushing them down or pulling them back behind me to get to open water. Where did all the people in front of me come from? I thought I was in the second row on the beach, yet there were dozens of people I was clawing through. I could feel the people behind me grabbing for my ankles, a common trick – pull the person in front of you by the ankles and you quickly move ahead of them. However, try that crap with a prima donna cyclist and you had better be ready for a round of mixed martial arts. I shifted my kicking pattern to keep my feet free. I kicked a few people in the process. Sorry, but they shouldn't have gotten so close.

After five hundred yards, the pack winnowed out and I was able to get into a smooth rhythm. During my training, I practiced not using my legs except to pass and turn. The strategy was to save my legs for when they would be needed most, the bike and the run. It was going to be a long day. Pace. Pace. Pace. Now that I was in open water, I stretched out my stroke and started bilateral breathing, letting my wetsuit-wrapped legs float behind me.

The course was rectangular, with the markers straight out approximately .4 miles away. After the first turn, I felt someone tickling my toes. A key strategy to open-water swimming is to draft off a faster swimmer by positioning yourself six to eight inches behind them. Like the bike or run, the person in front does a larger share of the work and the person in back gets a little free ride. I wasn't upset about giving someone a free ride, but I was getting annoyed with how many times he tickled my toes. I stopped abruptly and allowed him to run up into me. We shared an unpleasant look and I quickly resumed my pace.

The toe-tickler caught back up to me and I added a little speed to evade him. The extra push worked as soon as I was in open water. The surf was rough. Waves two to three feet high hit us on the backstretch, causing most swimmers to change their racing tactics. I started to dive under the water to avoid the waves. This required a longer stroke and more breath, but the reward was that the waves missed hitting me in the face.

I emerged from the water with wobbly legs but with all my wind and energy intact. I jogged up the beach, looked behind me, and watched the mass of racers heading towards the shore, flailing against the waves.

"Get down! Get down!" Someone screamed into my ear, causing me to turn back towards the racecourse.

A heavyset woman with chemically-enhanced blonde hair was pointing at me and yelling.

"Get down!"

I tried to avoid her, but my legs didn't have the necessary control to avoid her grasp. She caught me and pulled me to the ground. Monica Seles' attack came to the forefront of my mind. I had a stalker who was taking advantage of me on the shoreline of the Gulf of Mexico! Before I could even let out a good grunt, two more women accosted me and began to rip the wetsuit off my body. I noticed a racer next to me having his wetsuit removed by another group of volunteers. Within five seconds, the wetsuit strippers had my wetsuit off, the stalker lifted me back up off the sand and she pushed me towards transition. Running to the transition area past the beach, I remembered a similar event occurring at a friend's bachelor party, but those strippers required twenty dollars and a two-drink minimum.

My legs strengthened under me as I crossed the path toward the bike racks and the transition area. The efficient volunteers had my bag waiting for me as I approached the changing tent. The tent was filled with Ironman volunteers, like Nordstrom personal shoppers. My volunteer, Chet, helped me to a seat and guided me through the transition. The transition area wasn't very busy yet as I was thirtieth out of the water, but it was beginning to fill at a steady pace as more swimmers entered transition. My volunteer was ready to get me dressed quickly. I swear Chet was paid by how quickly he could get me out of pit row and back onto the track. Chet offered to help me put on my socks and shoes. This service was great. I suppressed any Al Bundy reference I could conjure up and allowed Chet to complete his work. He packed all of my swimming items into the bag, gave me an arm to stand up and pushed me out the door with a very loud "NEXT" right behind me.

Chapter Twenty-Seven

I mounted my home-assembled Capri Tomasso and pedaled onto the course. My legs felt rubbery even though I had tried relaxing them during the swim. It took a few miles to get up to my target speed. The air was very cold and I wore a sweatshirt that Jennifer had bought for me the night before. The extra drag caused by the sweatshirt made me pedal harder than I wanted just to keep at my target pace. Three bikers flew past me. Hopefully, my body would warm up soon so I could take off the top and go faster.

I spent my grammar school years living in Middletown, Rhode Island, a small Navy town on Aquidneck Island next to glamorous Newport. I graduated from a Big

Wheel to a two-wheeler in those years, although not easily. In the early 1970s, I rode my Big Wheel like the wind, maneuvered around curves in my basement like I was Jackie Stewart in Monaco. On the roads, I was a terror. I'd weave in and out of neighbors' driveways, flitting through my cul-de-sac on a gnat's path. My parents bought me my first bike with training wheels that year and suddenly I was slow. The Big Wheel generated more power than I could muster on a two-wheeler. I couldn't steer with the same impunity as with my trusty Big Wheel. Not to mention that the bike lacked the cool sound coming from its massive front wheel. No, I was not a big fan of the new bike. Most of my friends on the cul-de-sac were a year or two older and they were starting to zoom down the street on their shiny new two-wheelers. I just watched, knowing that I would never be feared on the road the way I was with my Big Wheel.

I apparently wasn't feared on the Ironman Florida race course either, judging by the nickname I was given over the next two hours -- "On Your Left." Cyclists, to inform a rider in front that they are going to be passed, use this phrase. Some cyclists use the phrase sweetly, kindly advising you of their position. Others use it in a condescending tone to announce that you suck. On this day, 770 people would call me "On Your Left."

A train of bikers passed me. Their wheels moved together as if they were delivering coal to Pensacola. I was alone. Six women named Jennifer passed me as we traveled along the 25-mile straightaway from the beach. Printed on the back of each racer's number is their name so that the spectators can call racers by name. "Great job, Jennifer." "Looking good, Jenny." "Jennifer, pass Trent like he's

standing still." Nice concept. The parade of cyclists continued passing by me and I kept my head down, trying to cut
into the wind and make the developing pain in my lower
back go away. I had four more hours to go on the bike. But
passing four hours was never hard for me.

I entered the Boy Scouts in March 1979 and the following week we went on a camping trip to Camp Yawgoo,
in southern Rhode Island. Almost immediately after arriving at camp, the older scouts began to organize a game of
manhunt. The scouts divided into teams. One team would
hide in the woods while the other team would try to find
them. Once a person was caught, three or four Scouts
dragged him back to the camp and put him in prison. The
game was fun because there were a constant slew of prison
breaks that caused numerous inane arguments. I was on the
team sent into the field first. As a new Scout I wanted to
prove my worthiness to my fellow Scouts, and remain alive
and in the game as long as possible. I found a good hiding
spot inside the wheel cage of the trailer that had delivered
the troop's camping gear. My hiding spot was a mere 50 feet
from the prison, and the hunters never found me. I was
tempted to break my cover several times and try to rescue
some of my teammates, but I knew that I was an incredibly
slow runner and I would probably get caught before I
reached the prison porch, ultimately sacrificing myself. No,
I would wait until I had the perfect opportunity.

It seemed like the teams changed. People who were
on my team were now guarding the prison and some of the
prisoners were my opponents. But I wasn't going to be
fooled by this old ruse. Making the prisoners look like the
guards was too easy to see through and they were not going
to get me to give up this precious hiding spot. Still later,

members of both teams began milling around the front of the cabin and then they set out into the woods. I could hear calls and yells of "Trent, where are you?" and, "Trent, you can come out now." How stupid did they think I was? I had seen enough episodes of The Dukes of Hazzard to appreciate how the bad guys try to lure you into a trap and I was having none of it.

The calls grew faint as more time passed. I hadn't seen a Scout in quite a while and I was starting to get the urge to pee. I crawled out of the wheel cage, stretched my back to relieve the stiffness and walked into the cabin. I walked through the front door and was making my way towards the bathroom when the assistant Scoutmaster, Mr. Walmsley, grabbed me by the shirt. Mr. Walmsley was a deep-jowled man with a gravelly voice, probably from a lifetime of smoking. He shook me once and said, "Boy. Where the hell have you been?"

"Right outside," I told him.

"Right outside where?"

"Outside the cabin. I was hiding inside the wheels of the trailer."

Now his face was growing red.

"You've been inside the wheels of the trailer? For four hours? Didn't you hear us calling you?"

"Yes."

My voice was getting weaker.

"Are you an idiot?"

From his tone, it didn't seem like a question.

"No, sir."

"Then why didn't you come when we called you?"

"The game was to hide from the other team. The other team was calling for me so I didn't answer."

The Scoutmaster, John Greene, a man I would learn to love like a second father, started roaring with laughter.

"Walmsley, let the kid be. Good for him if he has the focus to play the game and hide for four hours. Stupid as that might sound to us."

I think he was praising me and insulting me in the same sentence. Either way, I needed to pee and asked if I could be excused.

I passed the 75-mile marker of Ironman Florida and checked my watch. Just under four hours and boy did I need to pee. I always had the power to sit still and quiet for hours on end. However, I drank a bottle and a half of Gatorade every hour and my body was not sweating like normal because of the cold temperatures. My bladder was full, causing my eyes to tear. On some of our training rides, Dave Werbel perfected the bike-pee where you could hold out your knee and pee from inside your bike shorts while riding your bike. Dave was so proficient that he could hold 20 miles per hour while letting out a stream. Dave had the courtesy, or decency, to drop behind the pack to relieve himself. Now, I looked behind me, saw a wide gap and…tried…to…pee. It was not as easy as Dave made it look. Tried…to…pee. Nothing. Maybe my shorts were too tight. Robin Williams would have said that you could tell my religion by looking at the front of my shorts. I tried to loosen the waistband to give it a little more breathing room. Nothing. The Frenchies in the Tour de France must have a way of doing this and without giving the entire peloton a golden shower. I stood up in my clips and shook my hips. Nothing. Goddamn stage fright. Sure, Lil' Trent is now a little littler because he's been pressed against an unforgiving saddle for the past four hours, but come on! I thought of lying in the hospital bed and being catheterized and wondered if I could rig something like that up here. No thank you! Ultimately, I stopped in a wooded area and watched even more people pass me as I relished in my relief.

My legs grinded through the final forty miles. The highlight was that I passed someone while he was peeing, only they passed me again about three miles later.

Chapter Twenty-Eight

Chet was not made available to me during the bike-to-run transition, much to my chagrin. Lord knows that I could have used a little personal attention, as my back was stiff from holding the same position for six hours over the 112-mile course. This transition was less harried than the first because the racers, this far into the course, were much more spread out. Volunteers directed us along an entrance road where we would give our bike to another volunteer who, in turn, handed us our transition bag. My goodness, this was efficient! I grabbed my bag and ran into the changing tent.

During my previous races, I finished the run wearing the same outfit from the bike. This seemed simple to me. The sprint racers did the exact same thing. Something was different here. All the men changed out of their biking clothes and into new running attire. I laced my sneakers and watched five men of nearly identical build enter the transition tent, each wearing the same racing uniform. They were sponsored and working as a team. Me? The only sponsorship I had was from Adidas on my running shoes and I had to pay them for the privilege. I left the changing tent and onto the run course wondering what it would be like to be a sponsored athlete.

Baseball was the only sport I knew growing up, other than the playground games of hopscotch, red rover and farmer in the dell. I can't remember when I got my first glove but I remember playing catch with my dad in the street in front of our first house on Rosedale Court. Playing catch must have been very frustrating for him. It seemed that every other throw I made was over his head or below his feet. The most vivid memories I have of my dad playing catch with me was watching him running down the street away from me chasing my errant throw.

Baseball improved when I got my uniform at age eight. Now I was a real player. In my first-ever baseball at bat, I hit a pop-up to the shortstop, which was misplayed into a home run. I scampered around the bases as the other team sloppily threw the ball around. One player thought he was playing kickball and tried to hit me with his throw. The screaming was intense. The other team screamed for the ball and my coaches screamed for me to make my fat ass run.

Following the game, the dads drove us to McDonald's for a celebration. The workers at McDonald's must have heard about our rousing victory as they gave each player a free hamburger, fries, and a small Coke. The celebration carried on for hours, or maybe 20 minutes, as it was a school night.

The other team trounced us in the next game. Adding injury to insult, I was hit in the face with a ground ball, making my cheek swell three sizes. Funny though, after the game the dads took us to McDonald's and the servers again gave us each a free hamburger, small fry, and a Coke. Why we were receiving the winning treatment following our devastating loss? My dad told me that McDonald's sponsored the team and that they would give us this food after every game. A sponsor! I had a sponsor! I no longer felt like a three-strikeout, two-error, swollen-cheeked boy. I was a baseball phenom with a sponsor. The elation lasted all season. Win or lose, I would get the royal treatment.

As there were no other sports to play during the rest of the year other than 4-square, kickball, and crows & cranes, I couldn't wait to start baseball season again. Finally, the first game of the new season arrived. I picked some daisies in centerfield and thought about the free hamburger coming my way. Following the game, the dads drove a different route to McDonald's. But when we arrived in the parking lot, it wasn't McDonald's. I asked my father why we weren't at McDonald's. He broke the devastating news. McDonald's no longer sponsored us. This year, we were being sponsored by the Disabled American Veterans.

Well, that explained the large D.A.V. on the side of the side of the building. Inside, for the next thirty minutes, we listened to a one-armed Italian man recount how he rolled in tanks through Palermo with some guy named Patton. He gesticulated with his sole appendage as if he were taking on the Huns again. On the plus side, they did serve us apple juice. I guess sponsorship isn't all it's cracked up to be.

Still, I couldn't help but feel some amount of envy as the five sponsored teammates ran by me in their sleek matching running outfits as we approached the first mile marker. Just 25.2 more miles to go for me in my tight bike shorts and Day-Glo cycling shirt.

Chapter Twenty-Nine

I walked through the mile two rest stop, accepting Gatorade and a pretzel from an exuberant female volunteer. She was young, attractive, and had a booming voice that could be heard at the next rest stop a mile away. Along the way, I made a promise to thank each volunteer that I could. I wasn't sure what motivated these hearty people to dedicate a full day of their lives to us triathletes. It couldn't be for the joy of having our uncoordinated hands knock Gatorade from their outstretched arms and it couldn't be that they relished watching zombies march along with midnight approaching. No, something in these volunteers motivated them to care deeply for us. The young volunteer looked me in the eye.

"You're invincible," she said.

I was invincible. I felt invincible. My weary biking legs were gone and my fresh running legs were under me. The volunteer had hypnotized me. I was invincible.

I ran the pretzel across my lips and sucked the salt off the rod. I washed the salt down with my Gatorade and headed off towards mile three. As I settled into a comfortable pace, I thought back a few years to my kitchen table where Jennifer and I had discussed our desire to have a third child. We had two wonderful children and didn't feel compelled to expand our family. We executed the decision like a General Electric board meeting. "All in favor of the motion to have a third child say 'aye.'" Silence. "All opposed?" Our hands went up. The motion was carried by a unanimous vote, 2-0. I'm pretty sure the goldfish would have voted our way if necessary. From that point, it was only a mere formality that I would be the one to sacrifice my sexual organs to ensure the motion was sustained.

A month following my vasectomy surgery, I was scheduled to deliver a sperm sample to verify that the procedure was successful and that all the little soldiers were gone from my system. On the Friday I was to deliver my sample, I was heading to Vermont for my annual three-day golf tournament. My close friend Paul McGoldrick was going to drive and arrived at my house at 8:30 a.m. to head out. As he pulled into the driveway ten minutes early, my mother-in-law, who had come to take my son out for the day, followed him into the driveway. The normal family-of-four-shuffle-and-confusion ensued. I loaded Paul's car with my bag and clubs, kissed Jennifer and the kids goodbye, told my mother-in-law to have a nice day, and proceeded to leave until....I remembered that I hadn't made a sample. Uh oh! Leaving Paul, Jennifer, the kids, my mother-in-law, and the goldfish talking in the kitchen, I raced upstairs to, as my Catholic teacher described, "engage in self-mutilation." Unfortunately, self-mutilating was more of a chore than when I was a teenager, when you can hear the argument between your children in the next room about how many more episodes of Bob the Builder they are going to watch.

After a few minutes of futile effort, I realized that I needed some stimulation beyond my own imagination and reached into my wife's magazine desk on her side of the bed. Frustratingly, my wife didn't subscribe to sleazy magazines like Cosmopolitan with their "50 dirty things to say to arouse your man." Instead, Jennifer's stack contained cooking magazines. How the hell was I going to find something erotic about potatoes au gratin? After more minutes of frustration and hardened focus, I finally succeeded. I bounced downstairs with my sample in hand and a spring in my step. I sauntered by my mother-in-law, giving her a wink as I passed, grabbed Paul and left the house.

Once in the car, I told Paul that we needed to make two quick stops on the way. We stopped at Citizens Bank about a mile from my house to get some spending cash for the weekend. Paul parked the car and I proceeded to put my sample on the dashboard in front of him.

"Don't let this spill," I said and I left the car for the ATM.

Back in the car a few minutes later, I took my sample and gave it an overly-long visual check.

"Ok. Let's go."

Paul's face was puzzled and ashen. He knew that something foul had happened, but couldn't bring himself to acknowledge the uncomfortableness. We drove to the doctor's office and I delivered the goods to the professionals. I bid my soldiers farewell and went off towards my weekend of golf, beer, Wiffle ball, and meat.

On Saturday evening, I phoned Jennifer to check in (as all good husbands should). She told me that the doctor called and said that my "boys" were still swimming after sixty days and that I would need further testing in another month. I put down the phone, put on my peacock feathers, and strode into the middle of our 12-man golfing group.

"I am invincible!" I roared. "My boys can't be killed. Hide your wives and your cows."

Mile three approached and I couldn't remember what had happened to mile two. I think I'm going to finish this race. I feel invincible.

Chapter Thirty

The run course at Ironman Florida went 6.5 miles away from the beach, through neighborhoods, along Surf Drive, and into St. Andrew's State Park. Then, there was a turnaround point back to the beach along the same route. It was a thirteen-mile loop we would have to do twice.

The course was sparsely lined with friends and family of the racers as well as people who lived along the route. One house at mile four was holding a large party, blaring music from Black Sabbath. Guests of the party stood on the street's edge, offering beer to the racers and a respite from the running. The party looked inviting, the beer made my mouth water, and I could have tolerated the music, but my body was still feeling good and my hopes of finishing were high. I kept running. Although, it would be a different story when I ran by this crowd again thirteen miles later.

A yell from the crowd behind me woke me out of a trance.

"Make way for the leading lady!"

I turned to look and watched the crowd of runners behind me part slightly. Angelina Jolie...Michelle Pfeiffer...Meryl Streep? Which leading lady were we clearing a path for? A man carrying a sign while riding a bicycle approached and, sure enough, the sign read, "Lead Woman." Directly behind him was a thinly-built woman wearing an all-pink running suit with pristine white sneakers, who was running as if her life depended on it. Stupid me. There are no Hollywood types here. I just got lapped by a Powerpuff Girl.

Volunteers directed runners into two lanes. The lane to the left was marked for those who had completed their second lap and were ready to enter the finishing chute. In the distance, I could hear the roar of the crowd and the announcer's booming voice over the public address system. The lane to the right was marked for the rest of us who still had a half-marathon remaining. I looked longingly at those finishers who were two hours ahead of me, running on the high that their journey was concluding. Bastards! I took the right chute, had my bib marked to indicate that I was running my second lap and headed back toward St. Andrew's.

I heard people screaming my name at mile fourteen. Jennifer, her mom and dad, her uncle, and our sister-in-law stood in the street screaming for me. I appreciated the value of our names printed on the bib miles ago. Hearing my name in the middle of that drudgery created a surge of adrenaline in my chest. Many people over the past few miles had called my name from the street. I tried to greet each of them with a smile and a wave. With darkness falling and the number of spectators along the course dwindling, the runners were hearing their names called less and less frequently. My family's cheers made my spirits soar. I stopped and walked over to the team and thanked them for coming out in the cold. Jennifer asked me how I was doing.

"I can't tie my sneaker. The laces started coming loose a couple of miles ago, but I can't bend over to tighten them. Will you please tie them for me?"

Just hearing those words from my mouth humiliated me and made me feel like I was five years old again.

"I don't want you to get disqualified," Jennifer replied.

"Honey, if they're going to disqualify me for having my shoes tied then they can take me to Ironman jail now."

Jennifer smiled, bent over and tied my shoelaces.

"How are you feeling?" she asked.

"Starving. I could eat a whole cow."

Jennifer finished, stood up, and gave me a playful push.

"Let's go!" she yelled. "It's getting cold out here and we're not going to wait all night."

I shuffled off. My in-laws screamed my name in encouragement as I left their viewing spot. My face was long and tired. It resembled a melted Salvatore Dali clock. I could have eaten a whole cow at that point. Where was I going to find a prime rib on the course?

My parents had started a tradition when I was an early teenager. We would drive from Rhode Island into

New Hampshire on the Sunday of Columbus Day weekend for a complete turkey dinner. Green Ridge Turkey Farm was a vast, ancient establishment that served a full Thanksgiving dinner, complete with all the traditional fixings and topped off with a 9"-high baked Alaska.

At 17, my parents allowed me to take my high school sweetheart along for the trip. On our arrival, I took Paula to the turkey pen out front.

"It's cool that we get to pick out our turkey for dinner," I said.

There was an employee near the cages.

"I'll take that one," I said.

Paula's face turned ashen. She didn't know I was joking and thought I was actively encouraging a turkey execution.

In the year after I was married, I gained quite a bit of sympathy weight while Jennifer carried Haley. During that summer, I decided that I would go on my first diet and swore off meats and sweets for the next eight weeks -- ending, of course, on the Sunday before Columbus Day at the Green Ridge Turkey Farm. The world will not recognize me as the smartest dieter as I turned off meats and sweets in favor of eating three bagels a day. My weight stayed constant during those eight weeks, but I held true to the "diet."

The day had arrived and we prepared to go. For added pressure, Jennifer had invited my in-laws to join us. The pangs of hunger in my stomach served as a homing beacon as I gave my father in-law directions to the restaurant. Haley was traveling comfortably in her car seat eating processed peas. She didn't know that she was filling up on crap and that juicy turkey was only a few miles up the road.

We turned off the highway and headed down the main road.

"It's just a mile up ahead on the left, at the light."

My father in-law took a left at the light and turned into the parking lot of... Barnes & Noble bookstore? Were we in the wrong place? The restaurant should be right here. What the hell? My father in-law, who already had a marginal opinion of me, asked me where the restaurant was. I jumped out of the car and pointed at the bookstore.

"Right here. It has been right here for the last ten years. It's been right here since like the beginning of time!"

What had happened to the restaurant? My internal turkey timer had popped and I wasn't thinking rationally. Maybe a Nor'easter blew in and dropped a Barnes & Noble onto the Turkey Farm.

The truth was starting to set in. The Turkey Farm was no more. Plucked from life by a bookstore. Still, I was famished. My thoughts turned to the cooking section of the store. I just wanted to see a turkey. Pathetic.

My father-in-law quickly took control of the situation and said that there was a steakhouse only a few miles down the road. We all got back into the car, put away the razor blades, and fastened our seatbelts.

I ordered the 24-ounce prime rib and cleaned my plate within minutes. Then, I leaned over to my father-in-law and gestured at the three ounces of steak left on his plate.

"Jim, are you going to finish that?"

Now, nine hours into my first Ironman, I could eat a whole cow. I had burned almost 5,000 calories by that point. My stomach was growling. The lack of hearty nutrition was making me weaker by the minute.

I realized that I was at the moment of my journey when I would have to reach into my suit. The bike, the swim, and the run up to that point had pushed me, but not to my limit. I was tired and hungry. My mind was losing focus and I was ready to stop. A hitch developed in my running stride to accommodate the tightness in my back. I couldn't take a full stride with my left leg, which caused my right leg to swing a little wide. It was getting worse with each mile.

Why was I putting myself through this? What was I trying to prove? Does finishing this race matter to anyone other than me? I had ten more miles to run and it was dark and cold. I was ready to stop. Everyone would be proud enough of me if I finished now, wouldn't they? Dr. Iannitti would be amazed that I was able to run around the block that first day he told me that I could walk. Jennifer would be less worried if I stopped. She constantly pointed out that I was probably doing long-term damage to myself. Haley and Max were going to love me just as much tomorrow as today. Stopping here won't change that.

I stopped. I walked. I put my hands on my hips and watched people pass me. I felt humiliated and frustrated for quitting. Trent, you need to reach into your suit and see what you've got. My parents had labeled me "half-job" for a reason, because I didn't finish what I started. God gave me a chance, not for something as silly as an Ironman. He gave me a chance to make myself better. As I had reflected previously, life before the accident was easy. Finishing the Ironman wasn't the apex of my journey. Finishing what I told myself I would finish was the true value. Life had been easy because I had never challenged myself. I was now a stronger man and it was time to reach into my suit.

Chapter Thirty-One

I needed to block out the bad thoughts. Ten miles to go and the sun had set an hour ago. The road was dark except for the glow sticks the volunteers were passing out. A group of three runners had just passed me, their fluorescent sticks moving like dancers on Ecstasy in a rave bar. I needed a way to make another mile just slip by.

Working as a dishwasher in high school was tedious. Collecting plates, scrubbing them, washing them, drying them, replacing them, and repeating it all over again was mind-numbing. Often I would close my eyes and start playing an album in my head. I would turn to albums that I had burned the needle through like The Beatles' Sgt. Pepper's Lonely Hearts Club Band, Jackson Browne's Running on Empty, and Bob Seger's Live Bullet. My infatuation with Bruce Springsteen kept Born to Run churning through my head. And, there were times when I just wanted to pass time with one song, in that case I always turned to "American Pie."

"Long, long time ago..." In the year that I had earned the freedom to swim in my grandparents' lake with just my friends and no adult supervision, I had sung "American Pie" a thousand times. Connected to the beach end of the lake was a dock that protruded into the water for about thirty yards. My friends and I would thrill in running at top speed down the dock and performing cannonballs into the water. Cannonballs morphed into various ways to be shot and "die" into the water. We imagined that we had been shot by surprise, or shot while robbing a bank, or shot off our horse, or shot in the butt. In one of those variations, we included the lyric "this will be the day that I die" with a tremendous exaggeration on the final syllable. The game changed to us singing the entire chorus while running down the dock and timing our jumps to the word "die." Finally, after we'd exhausted ourselves running, we'd just jump from a standing position on the dock while trying to get out the entire chorus before we went underwater. "byebyemissamericanpiedrovemychevytothelevybutthelevywasdrythemgoodoldboyzweredrinkingwhiskeyandryesingingthis....blub,blub,blub." I can't honestly say that in my hundreds of attempts I ever got the whole chorus out before going under.

Those summer afternoons seemed to stretch on as long as the eight minutes and thirty-three seconds of the song. The mile 17 rest stop was right in front of me. "American Pie" passed the time again. The miles were moving at a better pace than I had imagined. Songs floated in my head, mostly snippets or hooks, and were quickly replaced by new songs.

I passed the Black Sabbath party. It was two hours after my first pass and the party rocked even harder. I knew the road I was running on now as this was the second loop. Knowing the road gave me the confidence that I could actually finish the Ironman. I just needed to make one more left. Then, just one more left. And one more left after that.

Chapter Thirty-Two

Illuminated in the distance a mile ahead was the finish line. Approximately nine-and-a-half minutes of running remained, accounting for my last store of adrenaline. The noise level increased from the desolate quiet of the park just a few miles back. More spectators lined the sides of the road, waiting for their racer to pass. They offered polite applause to the rest of the survivors. Then I could hear *the* voice. It was the voice my friends told me would send shivers down my back. Mike Reilly, the voice of the Ironman, was booming out another finisher's name.

"Theresa Perkins of Topeka, Kansas. YOU'RE AN IRONMAN! Mike Mitchell of Pompano Beach, Florida. YOU'RE AN IRONMAN!"

The chant went on and got louder as I neared the finishing chute.

The finishing chute, designed like a capital 'Z,' was about ten feet wide and packed with spectators on each side. Entering the chute, I opened my arms wide and touched the skin of as many screaming fans I could reach. Fans were screaming at me and I was screaming back. The pain of the last eleven hours vacated my body, replaced by euphoria. I imagined this was what one feels the moment before dying and seeing God: white lights, no more pain, and a sense of relief.

I turned the final corner, forty yards away from my goal and could see myself on the Jumbotron, my Day-Glo top reflecting against the bright spotlights.

"Trent Theroux of Barrington, Rhode Island. YOU'RE AN IRONMAN!!!!

"AAAAAAAAAAAAAAAAAAAAAAAAaaaaaaaaaaaaa hhhhhhhhhhhh!"

I pumped my fist in the air and flew across the finish line like Superman.

The Ironman folks processed me through the finish, took the chip off my leg, snapped my picture, handed me a thermal wrap, and moved me out the door to attend to the next finisher. These people were efficient.

I staggered for a minute in the glow, relishing the achievement, appreciating the journey from a crippling boat injury to the pinnacle of endurance sports.

My shoulders twitched and shivered. Throngs of people were pushing around me searching for their loved ones in and around the finish area. Racers piled up behind me. My whole body shivered and my teeth started chattering. The night was cold, colder than it was when we started the day, and my body was in full spasm. Jennifer found me leaning against a post shaking and she hugged me warmly.

"You did it."

"No," I chattered. "We did it. Thank you so much. We did it!"

Chapter Thirty-Three

Jennifer gave me a sweatshirt and headed off to find something for me to eat. I leaned against a wall and felt my teeth chatter. *I just finished the Ironman.* The thought made my heart swell with pride. My emotions, suppressed during the day while racing, erupted and I started to cry uncontrollably. I was so thankful to be standing there, shaking. The loudspeaker continued the roll call of finishers. I'm sure each had their own happy story. I pictured some of the people I saw on the course. People suffering through the day in pursuit of their dream.

Jennifer returned with a bowl of warm soup broth. (These Ironman people think of everything.) From the first sip, I could feel the warmth heading back into my body. I chugged the soup as fast as my tired body could accept it, got a refill, and let Jennifer lead me out of the crowd.

I was leaning on her now. My back was in complete spasm and I was making the "I'm a Little Teapot" pose. Jennifer was used to carrying the weight, but tonight I was heavier. There was little strength left in me to be of any assistance. We had over a half a mile to walk back to our condo. (These Ironman people didn't think about sending a club car for finishers.)

My strength improved as I teetered down the side street. The soup did its job in my stomach and my body pushed the warmth out to my extremities. My sense of awareness was returning to me as well as my sense of humor.

"That's three events down, Jennifer. One more to go."

She snorted a snort that conveyed, 'Keep dreaming.' We reached the entrance of the condo and waited for the elevator next to two young guys, each carrying a six-pack of bottled beer.

"Dude, you don't look too good."

Listening to him, I didn't appreciate what my external appearance looked like. I couldn't see the grease in my hair. I couldn't see the caked white salt around the sides of my face. And, I certainly couldn't see where I had drooled large portions of my chicken soup down the front of my sweatshirt.

"Man, I just finished the Ironman," I squeaked. "Want to share a beer?"

"Dude, you earned it."

The young guy smiled and handed me one of his Bud Lights.

Vanity and machismo were nonexistent at that point.

"Do you mind opening it for me?" The young man smiled again and twisted off the top.

"Cheers." The elevator opened and I guzzled the beer on my way up fourteen floors to our room.

A Wendy's restaurant was across the street and Jennifer asked me what I wanted.

"Two triples with everything, large fries, and a Frosty."

She left and I ambled into the shower. I hung onto the railing and felt the water wash away the salt. This shower was soft, softer than the irrigation I had received just four years ago. It was quite an awkward journey between these two momentous showers. I thanked God for my second life. Could the severing of my back have made me a better person? I cared more about other people now. I felt love more deeply in ways that were immeasurable on a logical level, but I felt it in the recesses of my chest. Did I always have the internal strength to complete this event? Heck, did I always have the internal strength to climb out of the bed? Maybe I did. It took a near-fatal tragedy to expose that side of my soul.

I turned the water hotter and felt the added burn across my chest. A running rash that had developed between my thighs was now burning. I exposed it even more to the water, relishing the pain. I could feel. My fears of paralysis lived alongside me every day. Feeling pain is good. My mind wandered to The List and the accomplishments made over the past four years. Nine of my items were complete, with only an unprecedented open swim remaining. Too early to think about that now, but tomorrow I would have to think about that question. It is the same question asked of all athletes, "What's next?"

Jennifer returned with the food and I will confess that consuming three thousand calories in one sitting had never been so easy. Damn to hell all the nutritionists with their vegan ways. A Wendy's triple went down my gullet faster than a Maserati can go zero to sixty. I licked the salt off my fingers after I inhaled the fries. Jennifer was on the verge of telling me to slow down, but saw the ravenous look in my eyes and went about getting ready for bed.

A wonderful tradition of the Ironman is for finishers to go back onto the course in the minutes leading up to midnight to watch the final racers complete the event. The lights will shut off at midnight. The rule is that if you don't finish by midnight then you are not an Ironman. The people on the course now have been out there for more than sixteen hours. Jennifer didn't think it was a good idea for me to walk the half mile back to the finish line. I was ready to protest until I stood up but involuntarily left my legs on the couch.

"Maybe we can just watch them from the front door of the condo."

She helped me off the couch and we made our way to the porch in the cool night air. From the 14th floor, we could see ants marching, all moving in the same direction. The people I could see had almost thirty minutes to finish. These people would achieve their dream of finishing. Looking up the ant line, I wondered how many wouldn't finish. And, of those I wondered how many would be willing to try again to feel the level of satisfaction that I did at that moment.

At five minutes to midnight, the ant line was down to a trickle. The large majority of spectators on our section of the course moved toward the end to find their loved ones. I saw a person in the distance moving slowly along the road. It was too far to tell if it was a man or a woman. They were alone on the road, moving slowly towards their goal. He, she, would not be an Ironman tonight, not by the race's standard, but maybe by their standard and certainly by my standard. Being an Ironman doesn't mean you crossed the tape in time. It means that you endured the journey. My journey over the past four years had been quite awkward, filled with passages of despair, hope, love, pain, fear, jubilation, and satisfaction. Would I be in that spot had I not been run over four years ago? Most likely not. Life is shaped by events both consequential and inconsequential. An evening's relaxing exercise turned into a mantra for living life to the fullest.

Jennifer came back to the patio; it felt like she had been gone for hours.

"It's after midnight."

"I know."

We both leaned against the railing, watching the remnants of the racers.

"I want to go run with them."

"I know you do."

"I want to be next to them when they cross the line so they're not alone."

We both knew that I lacked the energy to go back onto the course.

"Come inside. You're tired."

"You just want me to go back inside so I can complete the quadrathlon."

"Yes, Trent, that's the only reason I want you to come off this balcony."

I smelled a whiff of sarcasm, but my dulled senses were uncertain I had picked up the right scent.

I ambled into the bedroom and eased myself onto the bed. My back was throbbing. My left side was in complete spasm.

"Jennifer, I'm not going to lie to you. This may not be my best sexual performance."

I readjusted a pillow under my knees to relieve some of the pressure on my back.

"You're going to have to do most of the work as my legs are shot."

Jennifer undressed into her nightclothes. She left me for a minute to brush her teeth and returned to her side of the bed.

"I'm ready," I pronounced meekly.

"You may think you're ready, but it doesn't look that way."

"Don't let my looks deceive you, woman. You're about to make it with an Ironman."

"Hmmpf."

That was a sound an eighty-year-old man would make looking at the nursing home tapioca for dessert. "Hmmpf." Jennifer found the light switch. The room became dark. She leaned closer to me and kissed me on the lips.

"I'm proud of you."

She kissed me on the lips one more time.

About the Author

Trent Theroux inspires, motivates and moves audiences, through personal narrative, business anecdotes and his poor sense of humor. Trent is a Vice President of Finance, Graduate School Professor, Endurance Athlete, father and Activist for the Spinal Cord Injury Community. Following an accident which left him paralyzed, Trent created a foundation to provide durable medical goods for spinal cord injured patients and funded the foundation through an unprecedented backstroke swim into the Atlantic Ocean. Trent's story has been highlighted in radio, newspaper and television. Most recently, he was recognized in Sports Illustrated for his record 41-mile swim circumnavigating Aquidneck Island (Newport, RI). You can learn more about Trent at www.trenttheroux.com.

62897946R10117

Made in the USA
Lexington, KY
21 April 2017